Strangers in the Mirror:
In and Out of the Mainstream
of Culture in Canada

# Strangers in the Mirror

## In and Out of the Mainstream of Culture in Canada

Essays

*edited by* Sanjay Talreja
and Nurjehan Aziz

We acknowledge the support of the Canada
Council for the Arts for our publishing program.
We also acknowledge support from the
Government of Ontario through the Ontario Arts Council.

National Library of Canada Cataloguing in Publication


Strangers in the mirror : in and out of the mainstream
of culture in Canada : essays / edited by Sanjay Talreja
and Nurjehan Aziz.

Includes bibliographical references.

ISBN 1-894770-19-6

1. Minorities--Canada. 2. Minorities in mass media.
I. Talreja, Sanjay II. Aziz, Nurjehan

FC95.5.S77 2005 305.5'6'0971 C2004-905854-1

Printed in Canada by Coach House Printing

TSAR Publications
P. O. Box 6996, Station A
Toronto, Ontario M5W 1X7
Canada

www.tsarbooks.com

# Contents

# Introduction

## SANJAY TALREJA

By all indications, I am a "successful" immigrant. Barely five years after moving to Canada, I have a teaching job at a university, am working in my chosen field, and am writing and directing a film for the National Film Board of Canada. And yet when I look in the mirror that reflects Canada to itself and the world, I do not see myself. I see nothing. I don't see my Punjabi taxi driver or my Somali neighbour nor hear my daughter's Kenyan friend or my Trinidadian colleague. The radio rarely sounds like me or them, it barely speaks for or to me; on TV, I am virtually absent unless there is bad news. Sometimes I think I will feel forever foreign.

A few months ago, when we were inviting contributions to this anthology, I wrote: "Each day, I turn on the TV, listen to the radio, read the newspaper, and each day I feel more invisible. I look for signs of a healthy, vibrant, and diverse society but everywhere I look—in the media and elsewhere—Canada's much vaunted multiculturalism often feels like a tired and empty mantra." A well-intentioned friend asked me what I meant by this. Was any other place in the world as benevolent as Canada? Did I know any country that was as multicultural?

Multiculturalism. When I moved to Canada a few years ago, I was simultaneously repulsed and fascinated by the chanting of this word. I had lived in the United States for some years and had become angry at the unspoken, ordinariness of flag-waving, chest-thumping, jingoist ultranationalism and gotten frustrated by the exhortations of dissolving myself into the great red-white-and-blue melting pot. That was among the main reasons I left the US and came to Canada. Here I discovered that identity was defined by a multisyllabic word—mul-ti-cul-tur-al-ism.

Multiculturalism. What was this strange-headed beast? The longer I lived in Toronto, the more I realised that the term was repeated like a hymn at every seminar and lecture, pontificated about endlessly on TV and radio. Anytime a brown, black, rainbow-hued person showed up, someone would inevitably bring up the word and hold it up as the magical essence of what it was to be Canadian.

On the radio one morning, I discovered what it meant. "I eat Canadian bacon and eggs in the morning," one hip, twenty-year something breathlessly intoned, "do Indian or Thai for lunch, Chinese for dinner and then, in the evening, I groove to Latin and African music." Another interviewee was a little more articulate. "We're exposed to so much in this diverse country, so it's only natural that we're tolerant and the world's peacekeepers. I feel really proud when I walk on the street and see the United Nations. It makes me realize that we live in a forgiving society." When the reporter asked him to name some of his non-Canadian born friends, he hemmed and hawed and finally admitted he didn't have any. The reporter continued to press. Name one immigrant writer, artist or filmmaker, he said. Still nothing.

Let's pause a bit—admittedly, there is something useful in what they are saying even if they say it so blandly and seem naïve and unsophisticated; and I strongly believe that the reaction wouldn't vary too much if one went to any other country and asked similar questions. But to hear such immaturity on publicly funded radio after more than thirty years of official multiculturalism and education is something of a shame. Would I be wrong in asserting that, for many, this is what multi-cultur-alism is--catchwords and phrases, official mythologies deeply felt? Sometimes I wonder if our job as coloured folks is to provide the exoti-cism, spice, music, and passion, while English and French folk provide the values and leadership; together, we lurch our way into the brave new Canadian world.

To my eyes, there is a disconnect between reality and perception. A glance at busy city streets indicates that the number of mixed-race cou-ples and friendships is increasing but mainstream Canadian media bare-ly reflects that. While some Canadians talk about these things in private, the media seems to live in an entirely different world, projecting a dif-ferent self-image to Canadians.

The disconnect in the world of politics and current events is even more drastic. Discussions about Zimbabwe's history of white domina-tion are overshadowed by the righteous barrage on Mugabe's unjust tar-geting of white farmers; the so-called Shia-Sunni schism in Arab soci-ety is exaggerated in our press as if Arab nationalism did not exist; we hear little about the institutional bias and prejudice of Canada's profes-sional associations and the duplicity of our government in wooing for-eign-trained professionals to immigrate, only to have their hopes total-ly dashed once they get here; our radio shows are still about gardening rather than refugee and immigrant rights; the music played on CBC radio is overwhelmingly classical and European-based; on TV we still see curling, never cricket. From films to textbooks, from radio and tel-evision to magazines, the stories we are told, and those who get to tell them are very narrowly defined.

Some will respond by saying that all of this is impressionistic and hearsay and that they need concrete examples of deliberate ignorance and unease. But how does one document absences? The only thing that I can say is, look around: where are the serious op-eds about racism? Where is the information about the continued paternalism and offensive treatment of aboriginals? Where are the varied viewpoints, the voices of dissent, the markers that indicate that we live in a society where all kinds of people, with histories, experiences, songs, stories come from? Where are the conversations about who gets to write, make images, talk? Where is the dialogue about the policy mechanisms that have been created to encourage a broad presence in the media? Where is the debate about media ownership and representation?

The problem, in my opinion, is that many Canadians—those who work in the media, but also in mainstream Canadian society—are too smug in their multiculturalism, and so content that they are not ugly Americans, so pleased that they are soft nationalists, and so sure that they speak with the rational, objective voice of the sensible Western world, that they refuse to believe that tolerance, diversity, multiculturalism are notions that they, we all, have to constantly work to realize.

Last year, I happened to be present in Toronto as an observer at a meeting of the nation's top documentary producers. Practically every one of them expressed discontent at telling "little" Canadian stories and spoke long and passionately about wanting to do more international stories. Stories about the Arab street, or the tragedy of Africa, or the sale of Romanian orphans. Inexplicably, I found myself squirming as I heard them go on and on. And then it came to me. "Excuse me," I blurted, "excuse me, I simply have to say something." I said in my little voice, "I look at this room and keep wondering what is wrong with the picture. And it strikes me as amazing and frightening that, to a person, none of you speak with any concern about whether you have the right to tell these stories.

"We sit in what is probably the planet's most diverse city where over 100 languages are spoken, where people of all stripes, shades and colours have been living for at least fifty years. All of you say you want to do international documentaries in Africa, Asia, South America, but I would be willing to bet that very few of you know anything deeply about those cultures or even speak a word of their languages, or know about their politics, society or their histories. We all know that ignorance breeds the worst kind of fly-in documentaries. Are you trying to say that there are no filmmakers here in Toronto who know those cultures better than you do, can speak the languages, know the histories and politics of those places? You speak with a sense of such entitlement, as if you're specially placed to do those documentaries. You arrogate to yourselves the right to speak.

"I hate to say this but there is this little matter of Eurocentrism that seems to be the elephant in this room. I know I am painting you all with the same brush and you could be of any descent—English, Ukrainian, French, Italian, German, Russian—but I think it would be fair to say that you are all of European descent. I thought we've come far from the days when Europeans felt that they were uniquely positioned to speak on behalf of all, and claimed to be objective and feel totally within their rights to define the territory. I thought the days of Empire and Orientalism are long gone but I feel their remnants in this room . . ."

Suddenly, in the midst of this harangue, I felt tired and demeaned, as if there was little purpose in going on. More to the point, I felt quite surprised by my outburst, as if I had ruined this professional meeting with my tired, whiny railing. And now that I think of it, what was truly stunning was the deafening silence I was met with—not one word was said, not one person would look me in the eye. It had not been my intention to play the "race card" or deal the "victim card." But I wanted to remind all of us, myself included, that there is a world out there, and the world speaks and we fail to listen at our peril.

I am not trying to say that only Indians have the right to make films about Indians, that only Pakistanis can write articles about Pakistan, that we should ghettoize ourselves. I am trying instead to say that by allowing Kevin Newman of Global to repeat the same tired lines about Iraq will not allow for a more nuanced understanding of that society, nor will having to go on reading Margaret Wente about wretched immigrants and welfare cheats, or Rosie DiManno about the irrationalism of Islam, or Jonathan Mann about terrorist Palestinians or ungrateful refugees . . . nor will it help us understand our own brothers and sisters of Arab, African, and Asian descent who are here with us in Canada. In my mind, such narrow but troublingly popular fear-mongering will continue to marginalize significant chunks of our population who feel that whatever they do and say, their voices will not be heard. It hardly needs to be said that such indifference and arrogance will only increase the cynicism and anger amongst our communities and the distrust that many feel towards the media and society at large in their refusal to present things fairly.

I must qualify what I have written. Canada is not the USSR, where official censors lurk in the corners, waiting to send dissenters to the Gulags, nor is it the United States where one deafeningly loud drum is heard. And we all know that the nations that many of us come from are deeply compromised, troubled, often violent societies where stepping out of line is not particularly encouraged. But that is the precise reason why we seek out Canada. And that is exactly why we still have hope. I think of this country as an experiment where people come from every single spot on the map, where class, gender, religion, national origin, sexual orientation matter little as I look at the many-hued fabric of this, my new land. Our expectations of equitable treatment and fairness are not too much to ask. Is it a fantasy to believe that our sacrifices will have been worthwhile? Is it too much to hope that even if we disappear, at least our children will see themselves reflected in the mirror?

If the mirror does not affirm us, I fear that we will continue to hear nonsense about Haiti's failed society, as if black people are inevitably and always doomed to make a hash of ruling themselves, as if Haiti itself is outside politics and history. We will keep hearing blather about the luminous queen mother and the quaintly eccentric English aristocracy. We will keep seeing certain kinds of faces that report the news, write novels, produce and direct films, are interviewed on radio and television. Our daughters and sons will continue to wonder about skin lightening creams and the smells emanating from their mother's kitchens, and the kinkiness in their hair, and the unpronounceability of their names. Our schizophrenia will multiply even while we continue to mouth nice platitudes about food and colour and festivals and, dare I say it, mul-ti-cul-tur-al-ism.

Now a word about this book and our intended audience. First, our hope is to produce a provocative, discerning, fresh, and perhaps controversial look at some of the realities of our diverse country at an exciting, if also disturbing, period in world history. We expect the book to be used as a school text and also to be accessible to the intelligent general reader.

Second, *Strangers in the Mirror: In and Out of the Mainstream of Culture in Canada* looks at representations of and by minorities in Canadian culture; it is our intent that "minorities," "representations," "Canadian culture" be interpreted broadly so that some light is shed on these oft-used terms and our understanding of them is enlarged. Breadth of vision and risk in writing, rather than deep analysis is our aim for this volume.

# Introduction

We invited contributors to write about these issues employing personal insight, anecdote and analysis, in which history, current events and personal journeys met; through these writings, we hoped that the reader would acquire an understanding of questions such as: What places are assigned to various people in Canadian media? How do they fit into that unwieldy, ambivalent beast called Canadian Culture? Who gets to determine what is Canadian? And where do minorities fit in? In fact, what makes one a minority in Canada? Pigmentation? Birthplace of ancestors? Religious beliefs? Class? Recent arrival?

The essays in this collection are a mixed bag; more than anything else, we hope that readers can begin to experience the richness of timbre and voice in a country that is being minted anew, so to speak. Canada is changing faster than the mandarins in the academy or the politicians in their tents can perceive; the media is certainly lagging far behind in its ability to depict this rapid transformation. The sooner we recognize that fact, the sooner we focus on the paucity of voices and the quicker we attempt to correct those gross distortions, the sooner we can start working to build a truly egalitarian society. At its core, this book is part of a conversation with those who are aware that the tectonic plates of this country are shifting, revealing a vibrant, complex, dynamic society; at heart, the book argues that the multi-huedness of this country can only be reflected if the means and mechanisms, the forms and contents of representation shift.

Our selections are not homogeneous in any way nor do they pretend to speak on behalf of all so-called forever-hyphenated Canadians. While it is quickly evident that the essays in this anthology do not fit within the rhetoric of the official discourse of grateful, assimilated Canadians, neither can they be conveniently slotted as expressions of outrage and bitterness, nor are they laments of despair. In fact, they are hopeful, optimistic, and full of the recognition that Canada has to change if it is to be considered a vigorous democracy.

Beginning with a look at the Pier 21 Museum in Nova Scotia, important for the symbols it contains and as a symbol in itself, Sharon Lewis in her essay interrogates the national story this country tells itself and to the world. The museum's representation of how Canadians arrived to this land is far from inclusive. The beer commercial "I Am Canadian," which received so much attention, projects a picture of Canada that is all white. June Chua, in her essay with the same title, describes how her nonwhite features surprise people abroad when she tells them she is a Canadian. And Karen Kew tells us how in the eighties the Asian woman was viewed in Toronto as an exotic sex object.

The essay by Arun Mukherjee asks us to consider why it is that certain lives matter more. Why, she asks, after bombings in two geographically separate places on the same day, were Sri Lankan lives considered less worthy than Irish lives, by CBC radio? What does this mean for us as Canadians? Does it affirm racism? Or, hardly more forgiving, is it a case of wilful ignorance?

Youth. In Toronto, the ethnicity of youth is often conflated with fear. So, in the media, stereotypical Tamil gangs run the drug trade, teen Jamaicans are prone to extreme violence, the boyish Gujaratis are insular. But, as a teacher in a Toronto high school, Alnaaz Kassam sees young people in Canada as rarely portrayed on television and hears languages seldom heard on radio. Here, Urdu merges with Tamil, Pashto with Spanish, Tagalog with Gujarati; youths attempt to navigate their cultures and their pasts in a system that often seems confusing and indifferent, yet it helps create new bonds of community. Referring to Peter Mansbridge's extolling of young Canadians who fought in Normandy in the Second World War as giants, Kassam wonders if the young boys and girls who struggle in the school system to form the Canada of the future are not giants too.

In his essay, Chelva Kanaganayakam also examines the issues of youth, identity, and representation. He points out how complex the issues of identity construction and representation are and, rightly, poses more questions than provides answers. There will always be an "Other;" what is "home" and what sense of identity drives second-generation Tamil youth to volunteer in Sri Lanka? Why do the politics of the home left behind continue to matter, so that 50,000 Tamil gather in Toronto to express their views (to media silence)? Why do the youth resort to religious or "fundamentalist" self-representations?

In a completely different sort of essay, Fraser Sutherland tells us that the glue that holds nations together is not sealed in permafrost, and even seemingly static mythologies are changing things. Given the hoopla over multiculturalism and diversity, how do native-born "true-blue"

Canadians negotiate this world of difference and otherness that is now before them? Mixed feelings of being swamped by immigrants, feeling guilty through their consciousness of white privilege, the very real worrying over the loss of manufacturing and farming jobs, the contradictions of being poor and from Newfoundland and other thoughts are elucidated upon in Sutherland's thoughtful meditation.

Just as whites cannot all be lumped into one undifferentiated mass, nor can visible minorities. In an intriguing opinion piece originally written for the *Toronto Star*, Tarek Fatah writes how, as a secular liberal minded Muslim, he is angered by the narrow-mindedness of some of his coreligionists who see homosexual marriage as abhorrent. Why do these Muslims, who have often themselves been at the receiving end of slander and hate, asks Fatah, take such a bigoted stand? On the subject of diversity within a so-called community, Cecil Foster takes up the case of the struggle that took place for a black urban radio station in Toronto. He wonders, now that such a station exists, if one can talk of a single black community, and whether the station speaks to and for all black people in the Toronto region.

As in the case of the black radio station, the so-called visible minorities often have to make their own spaces in the world of art and communication, and to tell their own stories. Racial and cultural misrepresentations, caricatures, and biases have to be fought against; new and traditionally non-Western ideas have to be introduced. Rozena Maart describes the struggle for minority voices within a dominantly white art space, and its wounding aftermath. Robin Breon describes the public debate that erupted in the early nineties on the issue of the caricatured representation of blacks in the revival of the musical *Show Boat*. This debate echoed a previous eruption of anger over the exhibit *Out of Africa* at the Royal Ontario Museum in Toronto. Breon goes on to describe the growth and current thrilling renaissance of black theatre in Canada.

Rahul Varma, Montreal-based playwright and theatre director pulls back to another view. How do we understand the world and the role of art given the history of imperialism and colonialism, and the not-too-distant blatant disregard in the West for black, brown and coloured folk? In particular, Varma looks at the rapacity of large corporations such as Union Carbide which continue to thrive despite destroying thousands of lives in Bhopal, India. In our Orwellian world Osama Bin Laden's CIA and American benefactors fade from memory and the villain appears as unmediated evil. The destruction in Bhopal becomes a casualty of amnesia. How does an artist respond to the amnesia?

It is a tired truism to say that the terrorist attacks on New York City in September of 2001 inalterably changed the world. Everywhere, the spotlight turned on Muslims, looking for the enemy within or searching for the barbarians waiting at the gate. Contrary to what many pious Canadians believe, crude stereotyping was not the exclusive domain of our brethren south of the border. In newspaper columns and editorials, on TV and radio shows, in the image of the crusades, and in the dichotomies displayed between rational Westerners versus manic Islamists, we saw many blunt examples of Muslim-bashing. Looking at newspaper cartoons—things that we often do not take seriously— Mazen Chouaib shows how dangerous this Islam-baiting, scare-mongering has become. It reminds him of the crude anti-Semitism of a Europe of a bygone era. If we are not vigilant, Chouaib suggests, such depictions might become commonplace, normalizing hate and prejudice and creating deep schisms in our society.

In a similar vein, Michael Neumann examines the reporting of hate crimes in the *Globe and Mail*. He finds huge blindspots in its reports on anti-Semitic hate crimes; these, he discovers, get far more coverage than hate crimes that target Muslims. Like Mukherjee, Neumann asks if one kind of religious group is considered more human and more newsworthy by the venerable Canadian paper. What does it say for us as a society that we allow this kind of prejudice to go unchallenged?

What is it about the sense of foreignness? Is one always an outsider or does that feeling go away after a few generations? Will our dark skins meld into the great mosaic of Canada or will racism and a world of Anglo- and Franco-centric values always get in the way? When does one stop being a visible minority?

# This Space Called Canada: Re-imagining the National Story

## Sharon Morgan Beckford

For we cannot forget how cultural life, above all in the West, but elsewhere as well, has been transformed in our lifetimes by the voicing of the margin.

STUART HALL (257)

In the final analysis, the established groups have only one choice: to make room in all spheres of life for the other groups. This way, everyone will live at a negotiated respectable level of harmony.

CECIL FOSTER (23)

Therefore we can see the necessity for the kind of education for critical consciousness that can enable those with power and privilege rooted in structures of domination to divest without having to see themselves as victims. Such thinking does not have to negate collective awareness that a culture of domination does seek to fundamentally distort and pervert the psyches of all citizens or that this perversion is wounding.

BELL HOOKS (14)

## Introduction: Who Is a Canadian?

Last spring I had the opportunity to visit and learn about what Ruth Goldbloom, the Halifax philanthropist and principle backer of the Pier 21 museum, saw as Canada's Ellis Island. Visual images are important in this old harbour terminus on the edge of the Atlantic Ocean and the easternmost beginning of Canada. This is a museum that chooses with care what items and artifacts it wants to collect from the past and carry forward into the future as representations of our heritage and part of our cultural mythology. On a strong foundation, which is the past, Pier 21 and its financial supporters want to help us build a strong and glorious present and future. For me, as a visitor to this museum, a question that stays long after I have left, and is the original impetus for this paper, is whether these backers also want to build and talk about a Canada that is inclusive.

The images preserved in museums like Pier 21 do not merely remain there. They become present right across Canada and in our imagining of who were the early Canadians and how they are related to the Canadians of today. We see many of these images in sixty-second mini-movies, a form of government-and-corporate sponsored advertising that is intended to bolster our sense of having a common heritage. One such example is the heritage minute commercials, produced by Historica, an agency whose mandate is "to provide Canadians with a deeper under-standing of their history and its importance in shaping their future."[1] We see these sixty-second mini-movies ubiquitously on television and in the cinema. In addition, the provincially owned public education sta-tion, TV Ontario, has its own Trailblazer mini-movies, available to sim-ilarly owned provincial educators across the country. These docudra-mas of sorts all tell us about the great Canadians, the great things they have done and are doing, and how we should be proud of a collective greatness as Canadians.

In this version of the Canadian narrative, Pier 21 is possibly the most important beginning of Canada. It is also the beginning to a national story about those with an inalienable right to inhabit this social space and to jointly colonize the future in the name of a people simply called Canadians.

By gesturing to this landmark as Canada's Ellis Island, Goldbloom is hoping to return to a site that could be the start of one of the main narratives of how millions of people, born elsewhere, came to belong to this space called Canada. In American folklore, Ellis Island is the piece of land in the shadow of the Statue of Liberty where millions of immigrants, as the story goes, got their first glimpse of the United States of America and with that look began an inner social transformation that turned them into Americans. Ellis Island is part of the US mythology that speaks of giving "me your tired, your poor/ your huddled masses yearning to breathe free/ the wretched refuse of your teeming shore / Send these, the homeless, tempest-tost to me/ I lift my lamp beside the golden door!"[2] Ellis Island is part of the lore that "the land of the free and the home of the brave" takes the poor masses of the world, places them, figuratively, in the American melting pot, thus transforming them into Americans.

In Goldbloom's imaging, Pier 21 is the opening scene in the Canadian version of a similar story. This is a narrative of how so many of us became, and can become, Canadian citizens with an undisputable right of belonging. This is a story about Canada as "the true North, strong and free," a land which, purportedly, according to our official mantra, is a multicultural nation-state that draws from all the peoples of the world the immigrants who are then fashioned into its citizens. And, as a story of transformation and belonging, it is a social construction of all of those who went through the crucible that changed them from outsiders into insiders, from strangers at the gate into full-fledged citizens, from immigrants into citizens.

But while walking through this museum, it soon became obvious to me that something was missing from what Pier 21 was offering as a full story of belonging. As the artifacts and images on display revealed, what was being presented was a narrative in the making that spoke only about some of us. This was a narrative of a new beginning that, depending on the gaze, can be noted not only for who it venerates and honours, but also for who and what it leaves out. Indeed, in this narrative of the official beginning of Canada and its people, not all immigrants are recognized equally.

In a very short while it became significantly clear from the international and universal European representations—the national flags on display; the film on the reception of the immigrants from Europe; war brides from the European theatre of World War II; child evacuees from war-torn Europe; memorabilia, such as soldiers' uniforms, suitcases, passports, and letters attesting to European experiences that this museum did not represent the plurality of Canadian identities. In this museum there were gaps and missing people that are meaningful to a full appreciation of what is Canada, and whether the story of its achievements and progress is a narrative, as Stuart Hall states in the first epigraph above, that is in any way voiced from the margins of society.

Missing were images and symbols that place people like me in the Canadian narrative. As Hall would say, missing were the tales from the margin—the non-European world not part of the accepted mainstream in Canada. For example, what of the images of the thousands of Caribbean Blacks who would have passed through Pier 21 at the beginning of the last century, when so many of them came to work the mines in Cape Breton and to live in and around Halifax? There was also nothing honouring or venerating any of those Blacks who arrived in Canada from the 1950s onwards through Halifax, or those who stayed on board the great ocean liner and got off in Montreal. There was nothing about my relatives who arrived in Canada just like so many of those immigrants who arrived from Europe. Indeed, there was nothing in the images on display that indicated that the Blacks who have been living in the Halifax area since the 1780s had a part to play in welcoming these Europeans to their Canada. Pier 21 had very little for me, an immigrant Black female from Jamaica. Its images were about Europeans and the privileged positions that some specially blessed immigrants occupy in Canada and its stories.

## Images of Blackness and Belonging

As a museum, Pier 21 is a well-funded project that excludes a significant number of immigrants who came to Canada. Even if an argument could be made that certain ethnic groups did not arrive through the gateway of Pier 21, the Media Kit at the official website for Pier 21 states: "Our mission is to preserve, present & celebrate the *authentic* Canadian immigration experience" (emphasis mine). This raises the question: If this is the "authentic" Canadian immigration experience, then, of what kind are all the experiences of immigrants not reflected in the narrative of Pier 21?

Furthermore, how have those responsible for promoting *Canadianness* found ways to include or represent other arrivals? The experience of the Underground Railroad and the notion of the "Promised Land," though important and meaningful to who I am as a person of African descent, does not speak to my personal story or the stories of other Black immigrants who arrived since. Black people did not all arrive via the Underground Railroad, nor were our experiences of "welcome" a Jackie Robinson story.

I do not wish to be understood as suggesting that these stories do not matter, because they do; rather, the point I am making is that the stories of Black immigration are more than just narratives of "from slavery to freedom" in Canada, or about being welcomed from across the border. The story of Black immigration needs to include all the various waves of migrations of peoples of African descent. Finally, what is it that makes the experiences of Pier 21 *authentic*, what makes it necessary for those constructing the narrative to make a symbolic connection between those arriving via Pier 21 and those who arrived some 300 years earlier?

Rinaldo Walcott, also a Black immigrant to Canada, offers answers to these questions in his article "Rhetorics of Blackness, Rhetorics of Belonging." In challenging who gets automatic rights to be a Canadian, Walcott points to the Pier 21 Museum, refurbished and reopened on Canada Day 1999, as an example. In his examination of an article published in the *Toronto Star*, December 1998, he recalls the names of the many media personnel of the day—all white and mainstream—who entered through this "gateway to Canada." Canadians, such as Hanna Gartner, formerly the face and voice of *The National* and *The Nightly News Report* on CBC, Damiano Pietropaolo, then head of Drama for CBC-Radio National, Peter Newman, author and former editor of *Maclean's roman*, and former CBC president Anthony Manera all entered through Pier 21 (1928–1971). As Walcott rightly states, "These are people whose Canadian-ness is never questioned. Their ability to belong and become Canadian is not an issue of national concern" (13).

The point is that as a grand narrative of belonging in a country that is now officially multicultural, the story of the immigrants who entered via Pier 21 and went on to become outstanding Canadians is problematic. While it is important to acknowledge and legitimize our immigration experiences, the way the narrative is framed not only raises disturbing questions and issues about Canadianness and belonging, but also demonstrates cultural invisibility at work. Even to think of the gateway as Canada's Ellis Island demands interrogation. Canada, as a plural society with an official multicultural policy, unlike the United States, does not need an Ellis Island. The narrative of Ellis Island is for the American "melting pot" ideal, not for a nation where multiculturalism is the official narrative. Canada, according to official proclamation, is not a melting pot and does not aspire to be one. Canada is, in the official narrative, a multicultural mosaic, perhaps a quilt of many distinctive colours, a garden of many different and diverse plants and flowers. In addition, Pier 21 Museum requires access to a great deal of funding, which is not readily available to many non-European immigrant groups who want to write themselves into the Canadian narrative. Those who hold power and privilege perhaps should reflect upon Canada's goal, both nationally and internationally.

A rethinking of what is Canada requires that those in control not see the images and representations of Canada solely as theirs or about themselves, or reflect a perspective of noninclusion they may hold of others. Re-visioning our collective identity, in all its diversity and difference, requires seeing the image of Canada as multicultural. This would allow diverse groups to determine the ways in which they are represented on the Canadian stage, both nationally and internationally. What is necessary is a reconceptualization of who and what is Canadian.

Canada may be better off educating the Canadians who create its images and representations to portray a multicultural sensibility; this would help to eliminate the practice of writing narratives of exclusion, erasure, or invisibility. As Walcott maintains, and a point that as a fellow Black Canadian I share:

> What is at stake is a whiteness which can become national and therefore Canadian, vis à vis other differences which cannot. The kind of people who came to Canada through Pier 21 are rarely, if ever, questioned about

belonging to the national space by those who accept the official national narrative of nation-state formation. These folks are the natural inheritors of what Canada is, and they cannot only represent Canada in its national institutional spaces, but they can also speak for exactly what Canada is and means. They become ethnonationalist representatives of the nation-state (14).

The important thing I want to draw from Walcott's discussion is his notion that Canadianness functions on the premise of an "ethnicity-free ethnicity." This is a logic, Walcott argues, that makes the Canadian phenotypically white, with little room outside of official multiculturalism for imagining blackness. And here, for the purpose of this essay, I want to extend the definition of blackness to include all other marginalized groups that are not considered as white.

The important symbolic value that should be elevated in this particular immigration narrative would be that of multiculturalism. For Will Kymlicka, multiculturalism has an important symbolic value for Canada, which "had a history of racial and ethnocentric bias in the selection of immigrants" (57). And while this symbolic value may come across as window-dressing, Kymlicka's point is significant; the symbolism lies in the recognition and affirmation "that Canada is a multiracial, polyethnic country, in which full citizenship does not depend on how close one's ethnic descent or cultural lifestyle is to that of the historically dominant group" (57).

Yet we find that the rhetoric of exclusion is prevalent in media representations in terms of their portrayal of minorities who are "othered" (marginalized) in society. In portraying the mainstream as "the standard by which to judge or accept" (Fleras and Elliott 171), the media cast "difference," as associated with minority men and women, as social deviancy. Alternately, minorities are stereotyped in various roles according to old prejudices. For example, minorities are at times labelled as outsiders by referring to them by their hyphenated Canadian identities, such as Jamaican-Canadian, or simply Jamaican, Tamil, or Pilipino to name a few, even though the individual may very well be Canadian by birth. Marginalized groups are often cast as hostile and uncooperative with the police and involved in crime. "This reinforces the wedge between 'minority them' and 'mainstream us,' and too often demonizes an entire community for the sins of a few" (Fleras and Elliott 168).

7

The youths of marginalized groups suffer from this typecasting and the result for some is that they internalize the stereotypes circulated in the media and see themselves as second-class citizens or part of the underclass. Black youths, in particular, suffer from the stereotypes associated with crime and the ever-increasing, and perhaps misunderstood, *gangsta* tradition as popularized by hip hop culture imported from the United States. Images of Black youths in popular culture do not portray Black youths as being part of the "I am Canadian" image. This issue of demonizing Black youths needs to be redressed. Criminal and deviant behaviour of a number of Black youths is partly the consequence of what Canadian multiculturalism policy is working against.

As the multicultural commitment reaffirms: "Beyond the inequity, suffering and social disruption that intolerance and racism causes, Canada cannot afford to have any of its citizens marginalized." The social disruptions are a consequence of marginalization. A way of remedying this problem would be for the socially marginalized to see themselves as important to the Canadian body politick. As excluded individuals, they are alienated from society, yet they desire to find a sense or place to belong.

## Cultural Identity, Cultural Representation, and the Multicultural Ideal

Since multiculturalism was declared as the official policy in Canada in 1971, the notion of what constitutes meaningful national identity continues to be challenged by groups designated as minorities, such as Blacks, Asians, and Aboriginals. Today, in Canada, national identity can no longer be framed in terms of biculturalism, where cultural heritage is focused on maintaining the myth of the two founding peoples, the British and the French; rather, national identity and, thus, issues of cultural heritage and cultural representation have become more complex. The mass media have been criticized for not presenting a more diverse Canadian image that is not problematized by minority images that are "tainted by overt prejudice, open discrimination, and racialized discourses" (Fleras and Elliott 175).

Consequently, "minority" groups continue to articulate their concerns about how they are being portrayed, if at all, in cultural representations designed to develop and sustain a diverse yet unified national image that supports the unity-in-diversity claim of multiculturalism. While they believe that Canadian identity is a multicultural one, so that we can speak of Canadian identities, many Canadians do not see themselves or their cultures reflected meaningfully in the national images or representations in the mass media. Portrayals of minority Canadians, when they do materialize, tend to be framed in terms of the spectacular, the stereotypical, and hyphenated Canadian, who is perhaps best understood as the non-Canadian, or immigrant, whether born in Canada or not. Yet, this is not the intention of Canada's commitment to multiculturalism. The official Canadian Multiculturalism website explains:

> Lessons learned through experience with bilingualism and multiculturalism have taught Canada that acceptance and understanding of differences between peoples make collective development possible. However, experience with diversity also shows that inequities must be acknowledged and addressed for a diverse people to move forward together. This is a slow and sometimes painful process, but it is essential if all Canadians are to enjoy the same sense of belonging and attachment to their country.[3]

Therefore, it is important for Canadians to challenge cultural representations that do not foster acceptance and belonging in ways that are worthy of our claim and international reputation of embracing diversity. As Fleras and Elliott remind us, "Central to Canadian multiculturalism is our commitment to improving the responsiveness of our institutions to minority needs and concerns" (159). It is also important, at this historical juncture, to work at displacing cultural hegemony to allow for a positive reflection of diversity.

A beginning to making a place for all Canadians in the dominant narrative, in ways that are meaningful to them, would be to find new ways of re-imagining our nation so that a rewriting of the grand narratives can take place. Finding ways to see the potential in our nation will allow us to create narratives that move beyond the immigrant stories, to establish stories of citizenship and belonging that are not framed in stereotypical or spectacular ways. Our responsibility is to "uncover" things Canadian (imbued with a Canadian sensibility) and to disseminate those stories that will begin a process of transformation in the minds of our citizens from tolerance for diversity to committed acceptance, and thus reflect all Canadians. Canada recognizes its shortcomings and has implemented policies to address them, as the commitment points out:

> As with official languages and multiculturalism, Canada has learned that constitutional measures and legislation alone are not enough to assure equal opportunity in a diverse society. To contribute fully and achieve their full potential, all peoples must have a voice in society and a chance to shape the future direction of the country of which they are a part. This requires mechanisms to enable individuals and groups to speak out and be heard, and to participate in national debates. It also requires programs that help equip individuals, communities and organizations with the skills and tools they need to advance their interests.

The question arises as to whether these mechanisms are accessible to all individuals and groups. We know that there are power structures in place, with access regulated by those with power, and we know that funds are limited and carefully awarded. Minorities do not have ready access to the institutional power that is often necessary to secure an award from a foundation such as the Historica Foundation. But for meaningful change to occur, the power relationships need to shift from time to time to accommodate a variety of voices and to allow all Canadians to share in the opportunities of a diverse society that has its pride of place on the international stage.

## So Who IS Canadian?

As mentioned earlier, the images of Canadians in the media continue to be questioned and even challenged by minorities who do not see themselves represented appropriately, if at all. Fleras and Elliott maintain that "media representation of minorities border on the unacceptable" (170). Negativized representation of minorities is a systemic problem and although the media may not be deliberately disseminating negative images, "they accept, reflect, and do little to work against the ethnocentric assumptions of white superiority that are deeply ingrained in Western culture" (Fleras and Elliott 11).

A simple example is the Molson Breweries advertisements "I am Canadian," which depict groups of white males enjoying various social activities in Canada. How many visible minorities are reflected in the images projected of who is a Canadian? While it can be argued that Molson is appealing to a particular market segment, the symbolic value of "who is a Canadian" (or who is not a Canadian) cannot be ignored. This kind of advertising, Fleras and Elliott note, is "a symbolic and psychological form of violence," and is "based on certain assumptions about race and gender that are consistent with the notions that white males are superior [...] and [m]inority women and men are excluded from full Canadianness" (173).

As simple as advertisements may seem, they powerfully reinforce a particular ideology. Such representations need to be interrogated because of the messages they send. An inquiry into who chooses these images and why the absence of visible minorities is beyond conspicuous is necessary if the intent of multiculturalism is to be achieved. If members of the dominant group select representations of various ethnicities, then it stands to reason that various groups may argue about the ways in which they are represented or excluded from representations that lay claims to Canadianness. They may also disagree on how much the representations are a "true" reflection of themselves.

Indeed, because minorities do not have the power to choose the images that best represent who they are, the images chosen by others for them become "inauthentic," leaving them with a sense of alienation. Rather than being the subject that constitutes the representations, the "marginalized" recognize themselves as the "object" of representation and rightfully become disillusioned with the intention of multiculturalism. As cultural theorist Stuart Hall reminds us, "it is only through the way in which we represent and imagine ourselves that we come to know how we are constituted and who we are" (261).

In *Distorted Mirror: Canada's Racist Face*, Foster invites readers to consider this question: "How can leaders succeed in convincing troubled youths there are no shortcuts when they cannot at the same time assure them of acceptance as full-fledged members of society, no matter how well qualified they might become?" (23) This question goes to the heart of the problem of social deviancy. Certainly, the representations of Black culture and Black youths do not suggest that there is, or can be, a place for them in Canada.

Black youths have been demonized and stereotyped as criminal. Often in the news, the reports linked with Black youths have been associated with drugs and violence. Fleras and Elliott also make the point that differences that are "threatening or dangerous are contained, controlled, normalized, stereotyped, idealized, marginalized, and reified" (171). One obvious result of this type of distancing of minorities from the mainstream core is that it "drives a psychological wedge between minorities and Canadians at large" (171). This results in cultural segregation, where the negativized images of the marginalized are popularized and made to represent the norm.

Indeed, acceptable forms of representation are not simple to construct, because there are as many competing desires as there are ethnic groups. As Homi Bhabha argues in his essay "DissemiNation," the lived experience of all those who embody the nation is complicated by the perplexed histories of the living people, their cultures of survival and resistance that create a split in the narrative of the nation. Most importantly, I would argue that this split results in the ways that Canada as a nation is imagined and how we are therefore represented.

## Moving Forward: Toward the Transcendent

One of the things I would like to take away from Hall's essay is his notion that a culture in these postmodern times embraces popular culture, moving more toward everyday practices, toward local narratives, toward the decentering of old hierarchies and the grand narratives. This decentering or displacement opens up new spaces of contestation and, as he suggests, affects a "momentous shift" in the high culture of popular culture relations, thus presenting us with a strategic and important opportunity for intervention in the popular cultural field (256). Hall explains it this way:

> Within culture, marginality, though it remains peripheral to the broader mainstream, has never been such a productive space as it is now. And that is not simply the opening within the dominant of spaces that those outside it can occupy. It is also a result of the cultural politics of difference, of the struggles around difference, of the production of new identities, of the appearance of new subjects on the political and cultural stage. This move of difference [...] includes marginalized ethnicities, [...] feminism and sexual politics in the gay and lesbian movement. (256)

Thus, my argument should not be understood in terms of the either/or dichotomy, displacing one grand narrative with several competing narratives What I am advocating is the shift in a balance of power, a struggle over cultural hegemony. Cultural hegemony, according to Hall, "is always about shifting the balance of power in the relations of culture; it is always about changing the dispositions and the configurations of cultural power" (256). It is therefore important for the marginalized not to lose sight of the opportunities open to them that can lead to developing cultural strategies that can make a difference. This, of course, comes with the knowledge of cost, and the reality of underfunding or lack of funding, as well as the approval of those needed to recognize and accept these new strategies as a benefit to the whole polity, rather than as a threat. I believe that, in principle, the Canadian government recognizes the importance of "shifting the balance." Embracing diversity as strength would see an end to the practice of cultural marginalization that results in cultural invisibility. Since representation is socially constructed, and, as Hall points out, is an indication of who we are, those responsible for shaping Canadian identity through representation need to work toward dismantling ideologies that place minorities in subordinate positions in society and label them as the marginalized others. Marlene Nourbese Philip maintains that this is a form of management. Management, Philip says, is a way of controlling, "putting the unmanageable into preordained places within society so that they can be more easily controlled" (295). Philip observes: "Management works to control that which is considered different and representative of Otherness" (295). The "unmanaged" are those groups of people that European thought "has traditionally designated ... not only as inferior but also, paradoxically, as threats to their order, systems, and traditions of knowledge" (295).

Identifiable groups such as women, Africans, Asians, and Aboriginals, Philip argues, at times accept and use words such as "marginalized" to describe themselves. In this sense, Philip is referring to the ways in which language is used to control the way people, who have been "Othered," are conditioned to think of themselves. Thus, those considered as marginalized end up colluding with their own management. Rather than thinking of themselves as centre stage, they accept their position on the "margin."

Philip urges groups so positioned to think of themselves in more progressive terms, that is, consider themselves on the "frontier," and in so doing, resist being placed, or positioned, or "managed." Resisting management means resisting the imposition of limits, opening up new spaces of possibilities. Understanding language as the underpinning of power enables the so-called "managed" to reposition themselves outside of the relationship with the managers. As Philip puts it,

> From margin to frontier—is a deceptively simple act requiring no movement or change, but only a substitution of one word for another. It is an important and liberating step, this substitution of words and meaning, but to make the authentic leap from margin to frontier demands nothing less than a profound revolution in thinking and metamorphosis of consciousness. (300)

This change in consciousness enables the so-called managed to seek and find new possibilities and ways of creating narratives that shape new ideologies to support our diversity. Fleras and Elliott make the point that "If we fail to unmask the ideologies that underpin representations, we will be further marginalizing the people those representations exclude. Visibility may not be the same as power; that being said, invisibility is decidedly disempowering" (182).

## Conclusion

So while the Canadian government's efforts at putting Canadian multicultural policy in practice is commendable, it is not only important to "share our stories and perspectives," but also important to share power. The real change will come about when minorities are part of our political will, when they actively share power, in politics, in the boardrooms, and in various other positions of influence. Belonging is more than the "ethnic and the exotic" window dressings. Events such as Caribana, the Chinese Dragon Boat Race, Caravan, Black History "Month," the South Asian festivals, and other ethnic cultural events are now a Canadian way of life. These events are part of Canada's participation in the field of the "popular." While these differences enrich lives, the commitment to diversity should not end there. The commitment to diversity is most meaningful when it is reflected in who has power in the nation. Power is the main issue here, for "Until society sorts out who has power, and how it is used, and why it is used that way, and whose values will dominate, biases in representation will continue" (Fleras and Elliott 182). This essay is an invitation to reconceptualize who and what is Canadian and to advocate for constructions of cultural representations that reflect Canadian multicultural sensibilities. It is also about displacing cultural hegemony and a plea for Canadians and all media to value citizens as equals, entitled to the same sense of justice, belonging, and heritage. Marginalization runs counter to the unity-in-diversity claim of multiculturalism and disempowers some citizens.

Change can occur if we create a political culture in which there is more than just a willingness to understand the needs and interests of other groups. Just as important is the commitment to follow through with new projects that reflect our understanding of a multicultural sensibility. Yet, this type of change is not easy and can only occur with "changes to our education system, to the media portrayal of various groups, and to the political process" (Kymlicka 112). When Canadians look in the mirror of representation, they should recognize their diversity; there should be no strangers in the mirror.

In reflecting on the idea that in mythology the ending is merely a new beginning, it might be appropriate to return to Pier 21, this time wiser and with an intention to be inclusive. It may mean constructing a Canadian mosaic narrative, a quilt of sorts, that tells a wider story, not those carefully regulated segregated beginnings that we are passing on to the next generation, inculcating, subliminally, the idea that some immigration narratives have more social capital than others. Let's begin quilting, threading our stories to create a grand narrative of our Canadian mosaic.

## Notes

[1] See the Historica website at http://www.hostori.ca/foundation/about.jsp, September 8, 2004

[2] Excerpt from the poem, "The New Colossus," written by Emma Lazarus and engraved on the plaque of Ellis Island.

[3] Quote taken from the official Canadian Multiculturalism website.

# References

Bhabha, Homi K. "DissemiNation: time, narrative, and the margins of the modern nation." In *Nation and Narration*. edited by Homi K. Bhabha, 291-320. London: Routledge, 1999.

Fleras, Augie and Jean Leonard Elliott. "Miscasting Minorities: Multiculturalism and the Mass Media." In *Engaging Diversity: Multiculturalism in Canada*. 157-92. Toronto: Nelson Thomson Learning, 2002.

Foster, Cecil. *Distorted Mirror: Canada's Racist Face*. Toronto: HarperCollins Publishers, 1991.

Hall, Stuart. "What is this 'Black' in Black Popular Culture?" In *The Black Studies Reader*. edited by Jacquiline Bobo, Cynthia Hudley, and Claudine Michel, 255-63. New York: Routledge, 2004.

hooks, bell. *Black Looks: Race and Representation*. Boston: South End Press, 1992.

Kymlicka, Will. "Renegotiating the Terms of Integration." *Finding Our Way: Rethinking Ethnocultural Relations in Canada*. 40-59. Toronto: Oxford University Press, 1998.

Philip, Marlene Nourbese. "Managing the Unmanageable." *Caribbean Women Writers: Essays From the First International Conference*. edited by Selwyn R. Cudjoe, 295-300. Wellesley, Massachusetts: Calaloux Publications, 1990.

Walcott, Rinaldo. "Rhetorics of Blackness, Rhetorics of Belonging: The Politics of Representation in Black Canadian Expressive Culture." *Canadian Review Of American Studies* 29, no. 2 (1999):1-24.

http://www.pier21.ca/fileadmin/insidetemplate/inside_29.gif

# I Am Canadian

## JUNE CHUA

"Where are you from?" Such an innocent question. At a party in Toronto recently, a Russian émigré asked me that question and I said I'm from Malaysia. In the context of the conversation, it was benign enough. The person expressed curiosity about my culture. In most other situations, the question is downright rude and insulting. The issue of my nationality is never more an issue than when I'm abroad. For Canadians who aren't white, it's a recurring theme. After "Where are you from?" the next question is usually "But where were you born?" or "Where are your parents from?"

My experiences with those questions came back to me in full colour during the French presidential election in May 2002. Jean-Marie Le Pen won seventeen percent of the vote. Le Pen calls the Holocaust a mere detail of history and blames immigrants for rising crime. It made me think about how different living in Canada is from living in Europe. In France, where thousands of North Africans and Vietnamese have settled, sometimes a person would make motions with their eyes after I told them I was Canadian. They would ask "Pourquoi?" and make that slanty-eyed motion with their fingers. The question they were clumsily trying to ask was: how can you be Canadian if you look Asian? I always had to explain that my parents immigrated from another country. They would then nod, finally understanding my provenance. No conversation would be complete without those questions. To them, I was a Malaysian born Chinese Canadian.

The questions always feel like an insult, an attack. When you tell someone that you're Canadian or from Canada, they expect you to be white. When my friend Christine, who is Macedonian, visited Ireland, she was asked where she was from. When she replied "Canada," the young Irish man next to her bent his head low and asked in hushed tones, "Are you legal over there?" He wondered if she was an illegal immigrant. To the Irish guy, Christine's dark, Slavic features weren't "Canadian" enough. What does a Canadian look like? Pamela Anderson? Bryan Adams? I always feel a little smug when I explain that in Canada, when you get your citizenship, you are Canadian—no questions asked. That's the beauty of coming from a country of immigrants.

Because of my experiences, I won't ask a person about their ethnicity or place of birth until I know them well enough. It's a personal question, to be treated as delicately as the question of sexuality or how much a person earns. In Europe, concepts of race and nationality are entwined. That fact was made obvious to me when I visited my Spanish friend Macu and her family at their beach home in southern Spain. After three days of spending time with the family, eating with them, laughing and swimming, a heated exchange erupted between Macu, her sister and their mother in the kitchen. They spoke in Spanish and in angry tones that made me think they were going to kill each other. I felt uncomfortable sitting in the living room with her father. When the shouting ended, Macu took me out for drinks by the beach. Over beer, she told me they were debating my heritage. "My mother and sister believe you should say you'e from China." Stunned, I could barely sputter, "Why?" "Chinese come from China," said Macu. It was like a slap in the face. I had told them I was from Canada. They had smiled and nodded. I didn't think my nationality would cause such a furore. Macu understood the concept of immigration. Unlike most of her family, she had lived in other countries and talked to many foreigners about their own countries.

She took my side in the argument. "But, I've never set foot in China!" I told Macu. "And, I was born in Malaysia!" Macu took a drag of her cigarette and nodded knowingly. "They don't understand that. For them, Chinese come from China." She blew out the smoke. It was futile.

During the time I spent living in Europe, the question of my nationality elicited wonderment, puzzlement and sometimes ridiculous comments. Many Europeans regard nationality as an issue of race and birthright. I ask, why can't the person engage me as a human being without resorting to putting me in a box? Why does my ethnicity need to be established right away? In Canada, I could declare myself Canadian and there wouldn't be those rude, prying questions. I could be who I am and Canadian and no one would question that. But of course, it's never perfect. In the same week Le Pen won the first round of the French elections, Wilbur MacDonald, a member of the Prince Edward Island legislature, stood up and made a rambling speech, decrying the possible destruction of the white race.

"We seem to be on a track to destroy our society in a sense, especially the white human race . . . It won't be long in the United States when they will become part of Mexico and people from—I'm trying to think of, what's another name for the people of Mexico?—Spanish people. And I don't know what's going to happen to Canada." MacDonald apologized for his remarks. His comments aren't shocking, if you go back about 130 years.

Before the turn of the century, the Canadian government debated levying a head tax on Chinese immigrants. Canada's first prime minister, Sir John A Macdonald, said he believed the Chinese would always be foreigners in Canada. It has been more than a century since Sir John A made that speech and yet it still resonates today in people such as Wilbur MacDonald and Jean-Marie Le Pen. The good thing about living in today's society is that Wilbur was shamed into his apology. At the time of Sir John A's speech, there were no such recantations. The next time you ask someone where they're from or where they were born, please consider the context. It makes a world of difference.

# Today's Teenagers Are the New Giants: New Identities in a Diverse World

## Alnaaz Kassam

## Background

In a recent article (*Macleans*, July 1, 2004) entitled, "What Is a Canadian?" Peter Mansbridge described Canadians as giants for the population of Normandy. Mansbridge was referring to the 5,000 Canadians killed liberating Normandy from the Nazis during the Second World War. These were Canadian men who gave up their lives in the war. Some of them were as young as fifteen or sixteen. If we looked among our teenagers, would we find similar "giants"? And how does such a question affect what we believe about our Canadian identity today?

## Teenagers Are the New Giants

What is a Canadian today? According to Mansbridge in the same article, Canadians usually fail to come up with one answer when faced with this question. As a Canadian teacher in a racially diverse school, I often ask myself this question—what is the Canadian identity that is being formed in these young people as they emerge from high school, at almost the same age as the "giants" that freed Normandy?

The Canada of today is very different from the Canada of the 1940s—it presents a very different interpretation of our country than the mostly monolithic identity that existed in the days of the Second World War. As Canadians today, we take pride in the multicultural image we present to the world. The Canada of today is also a very different place from the Kenya that I grew up in.

In tracing my path to Canada, perhaps I can lay the ground for the complexities of the lives of my students and their attempts to forge an identity in this vast and expansive land that seems to lack no opportunity.

Growing up in Kenya, I had no visions of immigration. I lived in a beautiful country and I knew my place within it. In fact, being part of the Ismaili Muslim community, I knew my place within and without the community. I was born in the community hospital, I attended a community school, I would go to Nairobi University, but I was sure that I would eventually find a job teaching in a community school, attend the community mosque each night, marry someone from within the community, and live in a gated community which housed only its own members. When I got sick, I would go to the same hospital where I was born; when I died, I would be buried in the community burial ground. It was a safe and secure childhood stretching out into adulthood and old age, made all the safer because it was replicated by other communities: the Hindu, the white, the Goan, the Sunni Muslim. While it had always been community policy that our social services were available to all regardless of creed or colour, there was no doubt that we were privileged citizens in a country where social services were often left to the goodwill and resources of private and religious organizations.

Perhaps I failed to take into account the citizens who did not have this solid base of security. It was an environment where there were a multitude of cultures—but our multiculturalism was one of living "side by side" with others.

Coming to Canada, in the mid-'70s, as the result of political turmoil but also to get a university education, there was no minority community infrastructure to speak of. I studied in a Canadian school, I partook in Canadian entertainment, I went to Canadian hospitals when sick, I knew I would not be able to work in a community business, and there were no real mosques or even burial sites to speak of. Of course, much has changed now and there are established religious and community structures for almost all groups, but in those first heady days, it occurred to me that the future could no longer resemble the past, and it was very much my task to make the future upon which future generations of my community would depend.

What then is the case of high school students today—a time when communities no longer live "side by side"? Students, for the most part, attend the same high schools, live as neighbours, work in the same places, attend the same hospitals and form part of what is known as one of the most successful multicultural nations of the world. What is the Canadian identity that they form for themselves as a result of the landscape they find themselves in?

## Inside the World of the Canadian High School Student

In a recent interview, Rinaldo Walcott, a professor at the Ontario Institute for Studies in Education, remarked that Canadian multiculturalism as defined in government documents could not hold a candle to the multiculturalism that was being created by the youth growing up together in Canadian neighbourhoods and high schools, sharing space, music, and cultures, out of which would come a new society—a dynamic one where each culture would influence the other, thereby forging a new Canadian identity.

I have taught in four different high schools, and my observations here are based upon an amalgam of experiences. What is it that strikes one the most when one walks down the corridors of a Toronto high school? At one level, Walcott seems to be right—teenagers of diverse backgrounds mill together, dressed in the uniform jeans and T-shirt, boys in hair combed back with gel, girls in spaghetti-strapped tops that vie for boys' attentions.

A typical lunch hour scene might include the following:

A group of Gujarati boys huddled over a game of chess in a classroom supervised by a teacher, arguing loudly in their own language. Their conversation is disturbed occasionally by a group of white boys and girls who sit on the floor just outside the classroom, loud music blasting from their boombox, munching on their sandwiches.

On the first floor, near the gym is a group of six white students: three boys and three girls at horseplay and mutual teasing. A group of Sri Lankan, Indian and white boys, eat together and discuss sports. Near the auditorium sits a group of Chinese boys: they seem to be discussing music, tests, and teachers. A group of Philippino and white boys listen to their respective walkmans, occasionally opening their mouths to eat and discuss the latest movie. In the music hall sit a few black and Chinese boys who have their books open but are talking feverishly. In the upstairs corridor, a little away from my own classroom, I can hear Afghan and Pakistani students exchanging jokes in Urdu.

On the surface, it would seem that the different cultures no longer sit side by side but merge to form new groupings with much in common that they draw from a common youth culture. And to a certain extent this is true. However, as a teacher I come to be aware of the subtle retention of students' own traditional cultures despite the notion that it is not cool to be different. Indian and Tamil movies are always a big source of conversation. The corridors of our schools echo with conversations in Hindi, Gujarati, Tamil, Farsi, Dari, Urdu, Arabic, Cantonese, Mandarin, etc.

There are other themes that emerge in conversation with individual students. Some of the girls in my school welcome the fact that their parents will choose their spouses for them through the traditional arranged-marriage system, while others dread this. Some confide to me that they wish their parents did not attach importance to image and were more open. Most are extremely attached to their religious heritage and celebrate festivals openly—arriving in traditional costumes on special occasions. A few students state openly that they no longer believe in religion because it was the cause of conflict in their home countries.

It is in these conversations that the reality of these students emerges. There are several themes that weave a common thread through the cultural identities of my newly arrived Canadian students.

## Changing Families

It is not unusual to hear that a young student has to work to support his family. Recently a student confided to me that his father had lost both his legs to a land mine and therefore stays home and occupies himself with reading the community newspaper. This student and his brother work at restaurants after school to make money so that the family can survive. A girl tells me her father was killed in Sri Lanka, and now her mother and siblings live with their aunt and uncle in an apartment close by. A similar vein runs through the lives of students from other places—war has destroyed families, their health and their wealth, Canada is their refuge.

Another student's parents confide in me during parents' night. They were both surgeons in a major hospital in China, but for the sake of their single child, a son, they emigrated to Canada. Both do menial labour, the father taking courses to upgrade for a medical technician position. Both smile broadly when I speak of their sacrifice.

"It is all worth it for the children," they say. Their son graduated with nineties and has applied to the Ivy League colleges in the United States.

Another parent, a father, proud but angry at his daughter's marks, seems to have a similar story. They have emigrated from comfortable lives in a sprawling house in Karachi to live in a cramped apartment building where even the washing machine has broken down—only to discover that their child is not the prodigy they thought, and in fact may even have a learning disability. This father cannot find work in his own profession but stays at home to do the housework, while his wife who has never worked before goes out to a factory each day to help make ends meet.

These students of diverse ethnic and socio-political backgrounds form part of the new Canada. It is a Canada that rejects their parents' skills and professional backgrounds and forces them to work for low wages and live in places where more and more young men express their frustrations through violence. Students confide in me that mothers who have never known anything but the sanctity and safety of their homes and temples, where the extended family reigned, are now forced to go to work because they are able to find work more easily than their husbands. In such families the dynamics change, and suddenly, the girl child becomes responsible for child care and housework after school.

## Changing Students

Most of my students arrive from traditional schooling backgrounds where teachers reign supreme. Students work hard, and parents pay fees. Universal education is not the norm, and attendance in school is contingent upon performance. In the lax discipline environment of Canadian schools, where teachers assume that teenagers cannot be controlled, and where the culture is one of "school is not cool," there is much confusion on how one should behave. Immigrant students are often caught up in this teenage culture, not appreciating the fact that education is the only route out of a lifetime of poverty. While these students might have enjoyed a higher socio-economic status in their home countries, that status no longer exists in Canada. Others are confused because they have lived all their lives in refugee camps or running from one village to another, avoiding bombs and armies, seeking refuge. Now the lack of rules and the emphasis on freedom provides no structure, which they crave. Clear rules and clear cultural norms would allow these students to adapt more quickly and easily without having to experiment.

The numerous options available to teenagers in North America provide paths that can be confusing, leading to choices that bring easy wealth through drug trafficking and crime. Young women who in their home countries might have moved from the security of their parents' homes to the security of their in-laws' homes, now face daunting choices in their everyday lives in high school.

## Changing Communities

Unlike the situation that existed when I arrived in the '70s, most ethnic and religious communities are well established in Canada. Most of my students attend mosque, temple, or church and enjoy that involvement. Most retain their love of traditional food, dance, and music. Their language is extremely important to them and they speak fervently of retaining their identity through their language. However, traditional community leaders acknowledge that there is no hope for their kids unless they are educated and prepared in the ways of the host culture. These traditional communities are themselves grappling with change: how do they deal with the changing role of women, the need for educated men and women to take leadership roles and thereby change the customs of the old communities? How can communities deal with the diverse needs of their varied constituents? It is now no longer surprising to find that mosques and temples are multicultural realities with people of different nationalities, languages, and ethnicities sharing a common religious space.

## Changing Schools

Teaching in a school in Toronto is both exciting and challenging. On the one hand, it is a coming together of cultures with a speed and depth that is unprecedented in human history. It is always a wonder for me to observe how easily the young adapt to each other, creating new cultures by combining dance, music, dress, language, and even MSN to form new forms of communication and meaning-making. However, it is also a challenge to move away from teaching Shakespeare and Robertson Davies (with more than thirty years of department resources to support this literature) to teaching Tagore and Vassanji. And it is interesting that even though our Bengali student might find Tagore closer to his identity, the vast majority who are not Bengali struggle with the cultural and political context that is totally alien to them. It is assumed that when students come to Canadian schools, to be called educated they must learn Shakespeare and Davies. Learning the traditional Canadian and British authors is part of the process of being educated.

As the Toronto Board struggles with these issues and makes valiant attempts to include all cultural heritages in the literature we study, they are occasionally met with resistance from those who doubt the validity of the new and more unfamiliar literature.

## Changing Technologies

In a recent in-class survey of approximately ninety students, I asked how many of them had access to high-speed Internet. All but a handful acknowledged that they did. When asked what they used it for, most answered that it was for on-line chat purposes. Access was twenty-four hours a day, replacing the need for the ubiquitous telephone of the old days for teenagers. Subjects of conversations were all the things that teenagers talk about: homework, parents, boyfriends, school, etc. They have developed a vocabulary all their own that youth all over the world share. Individual groups of students might also develop a language that makes sense to their members only.

My students speak of communicating with each other on MSN, the lingo seeping into their writing for formal essays. Some students speak of "conversing" with cousins in Pakistan, Australia, and England. They download music in all languages, the most visited websites being those of Bollywood and the Tamil movie industry.

Increasingly, technology forms part of teenage life in a way that the baby boomers cannot comprehend—it offers an alternative way of communicating that the teenagers of the '60s would have envied. But while the teenage and early twenties of the baby boom generation were spent attempting to improve the state of the world, the teenagers of today seem to wish to shop and play games and listen to music; activists among them do exist, and the Internet then becomes a powerful tool to organize.

## Changing Media?

As I sit and write this, I think of the hours of television-viewing, newspaper-reading and literature I experience each day, and I can say with all honesty that the reality of these teenagers is not revealed there by any means. I think of CBC TV, I think of Book Television, I think of TVOntario, the *Globe and the Mail* and the *Toronto Star*—none of them are interested in these student. Yes, we mention them in passing, but only as exotic figures that cannot possibly inhabit the pages devoted to politics, business, the arts. This can be said to be true of all teenagers, but at least the cultural heritage of their ancestors, consisting of Shakespeare, classical music, the Beatles, the Bible, permeates all of our everyday conversation and our intellectual discourse. Are we asking that these teenagers, who bear the scars of war, of economic inequality, of broken homes, and of hurt societies, now close themselves off from the lessons learned and enter a world of consumerism to which they give themselves with abandon? Are we also saying that the cultures they bring with them have no validity in the largely Western European heritage that forms the basis of Canadian cultural identity?

Are we saying that the democratic structures that Canada has created have no room for these new identities?

Surely, the wisdom which these students bring to our shores, their knowledge of disempowerment and injustice, cultures and languages, and the value of civic societies must contribute to make a Canada that continues to be an example of inclusiveness for the world?

## Conclusion

I started this paper by referring to a statement by Mansbridge in which he referred to the teenagers who fought to free Normandy as giants. As I reflect upon my students, I see that they are just as young, but they bear the burden of supporting their families, acquiring an education, and building their own families and communities, thereby creating a new, tolerant civic society. It occurs to me that these young people with all their responsibilities for the future are also giants.

It is the task of teachers, politicians, health practitioners, cultural purveyors, and the media to clear the path and provide the resources for these young people to create their new world. Sharing resources will not be easy, for we have grown used to identities that define our Canadianness in set ways. But share we must, lest we become side-by-side multiculturalists, living in gated communities, protecting our own.

As Walcott says, "Justice is about ethics—at least it should be—not identity claims."

## References

Mansbridge, Peter, "What is a Canadian?" *Macleans Magazine*, July 1, 2004.

Walcott, Rinaldo, "MISCOGNITIONS: Or why I can't seem to get along with white boys," *Fuse Magazine*, 23, no.1

Walcott, Rinaldo, "What is the future of Canadian multiculturalism?" http://www.oise.utoronto.ca/experts/october2003/index.html

# Pictures at an Exhibition

## FRASER SUTHERLAND

### A Tank of Gas

Once upon a winter we pulled into the yard of a gas station. Wind flung snow around the yard in a perfect picture of white Canadian suburban desolation. Only the squat pumps were definable in the squall. From a faintly glimpsed shelter, hurriedly weaving through the gusts and flurries, came the dark, thickly clad man to pump our gas. He wore a mauve turban.

Piecing apart this scene, why should this be surprising? The turban marked the man as a Sikh and turbans are what Sikh men wear. He was only doing what gas jockeys and grease monkeys routinely do across the nation—though most of them do not wear turbans. For all I knew, a turban was just as practical a headgear in cold weather as a tuque. Yet, even taking all this into account, the scene seemed aptly emblematic: a spot of alien colour in a white field.

To abstract this picture, retain this image, extrapolate it to include a set of people, is to convert human beings into objects. This is standard artistic practice; it is not a good policy if one wants to nurture or sustain a human relationship. Between New Canadians considered as human beings and the images and terminology Old Canadians devise for them yawns a canyon into which we all fall. Or perhaps we stand on opposite sides of the canyon, staring across the gap. I personally think that Canadians have generous, kindly instincts toward newcomers. What we lack is imagination. We find it hard to hold simultaneously in the mind difference, otherness, and the overarching humanity we all share. With muddled good intentions, we substitute what we say for what we do.

## Themes in Search of Variations

If every culture has a set of self-defining myths, Canadians can be accused of boring themselves to death with self-imposed received truths. Until the end of the 1970s, and often afterwards, they seemed to be truisms. We're shaped by the vast spaces of geography, enveloped by a continent. We are a mosaic, not a melting pot. We refused the American Revolution at the price of remaining colonial, always looking to others for our validation. Indians and Eskimos, a.k.a. First Nations and Inuit, are victims; in fact, everyone's a victim. We live in terror of nature and of the North. We live next to an elephant, the United States, that's always about to roll over on us. The French and English are Two Solitudes. We're a new country.

Some of these ideas were disseminated by the literary critic Northrop Frye and his students, including Margaret Atwood, whose 1972 period piece *Survival: A Thematic Guide to Canadian Literature,* vulgarized some of Frye's archetypes. (To newcomers with fresh memories of massacres, the notion of "survival" in connection with the Canadian past or present must have seemed hilarious, if not offensive.) Since the 1970s, immigrants have redrawn the map of CanLit, and placed a diverse overlay over what seemed to be the Precambrian bedrock of our culture and society. Immigrants began to comprise significant voting blocks, largely to the benefit of the Liberal Party which, in governing in the 1950s, began to leave the immigration door ajar. Corporate officers with strange-sounding names began to seed the notices of newspaper business pages. Here comes everybody. The old, rural-origin Chinese were succeeded by urbanites from Hong Kong, and simulacra of small foreign cities sprang up, composed of Iranians, Jamaicans, Vietnamese, and Indians ("elephant Indians," in the distinction made by a Mik'maq friend of mine, not "feather Indians"). Our language changed. Use of the N-word ("nigger") became far more taboo than the F-word ("fuck"). No one dared to tell Polish or Paki jokes anymore, though Newfie jokes remained admissible. Simultaneously, long-established and long-shabbily-treated minorities, such as Blacks, Indians, Eskimos, and Métis, gained cultural, if not economic, ground. Indians were renamed "Native Peoples" or "First Nations." Dictionaries grappled with new, or old, nomenclature. Eskimos became the Inuit and spoke Inuktitut. Meanwhile, the sons and daughters from older generations of immigrants—Chinese, Ukrainians, the war-interned Japanese, the Italians, the Portuguese—discovered Pride. Everyone had a Proud Heritage and Tradition except White Anglo-Saxon Protestants, who had a shameful one.

Those were broad trends. In literature, immigrants like Michael Ondaatje, Rohinton Mistry, and M G Vassanji reaped prizes, critical acclaim, and wide readership. In their poetry and fiction, immigrants write about old homelands, and the experience of living in a new country. But they write relatively little about those for whom Canada is an old country. And the Canadians whose families have long resided here have no compunction about writing about citizens of foreign countries, but typically avoid artistically coming to terms with those who have settled here. To some extent, this is explicable. Writers are supposed to deal with what they know (though writing about what they don't know may be equally valuable advice), or perhaps, in the case of the native-born, they may worry that they could stand accused of indulging in patronizing or, worse, ignorant cultural appropriation. Is it possible that both groups fear engaging with each other in art, a mirror image of the lack of engagement in life?

## Designer Ethnics

Fifty years ago the WASP housewife, taking her life in her hands, would daringly rub a lone clove of garlic inside a salad bowl. Then the food revolution arrived in North America, as did the Food Network, dedicated to making us intimate with African, Thai, or Hispanic cuisine. Our rural or suburban housewife and househusband now toss whole bulbs of garlic into the pot, ladle on the *nuoc mam,* concoct incendiary curries. Dining out, urban whites stalk out of any restaurant in which white customers outnumber Asians, sternly refuse knife and fork in favour of chopsticks, and suspiciously eye the handwritten Mandarin offerings on the wall, fearing that the Chinese diners may be getting something better than what's on the printed English menu. Who says there isn't such a thing as progress?

Koreatown and Little India have joined Chinatown and Little Italy. When we old-style Canadians visit them, are we slumming? Are we there to be served by coolies and wallahs? Are the people in them only designer ethnics, whose role is to brighten our pale lives?

## Monoculture, Biculture, Multiculture

Both conservatives and liberals share the assumption that Canada is a vulnerable society. To liberals, especially those leaning leftward, Canada is under permanent siege by the United States and its global hegemony. To conservatives, Canada has abandoned its traditional Anglo-American values and institutions in favour of a formless, politically correct multiculturalism whose natural constituencies are in fact ghettos of festering enmities or whining grievances, and whose denizens are loyal only to race and religion. Some widely assorted practices or prospects function as flashpoints for their fears: female circumcision, arranged marriages for young girls, the possibility that sharia law could come into force. They deplore what seem to be immigrants' willful ignorance of Canadian history and traditions (though in fact the long-established don't know much about them either.) A conservative, or even a liberal, will smile knowingly when a New Canadian shopkeeper attempts to bribe a city health inspector, forgetting that for Old Canadians, too, bribery has long been a way of life—only they've done it much more subtly and on a larger scale.

Large- and small-l liberals might seem better predisposed to immigration as such, and give easy lip-service to piously hopeful terminology. We are a "new country." Or are we? Europeans began to settle permanently here in the early seventeenth century, and in any case the northern part of North America had been inhabited by indigenous peoples for millenia. Even if we only speak of Confederation, which established a nation-state in 1867, Canada as a stable continuous political unit is in fact older than many countries.

Canada, it used to be said, had two "founding peoples," the French and English. Now it is "a nation of immigrants." True, what became Canada was settled, in more or less chronological order, by Norman peasants, Scots-Irish refugees from the American Revolution, and uprooted Scots crofters. Ukrainians busted sod on the prairies. Coolies helped build the Canadian Pacific Railway, and later became the sole purveyors of anything that was fit to eat in Prairie hamlets ("Chinese & Canadian Food"). Blacks—first as refugees from the American Revolution, then via the Underground Railroad as escaped slaves, finally as immigrants from the West Indies, notably Jamaica—formed a low-paid labour pool. Battling more or less polite anti-Semitism, Jews entered commerce, the arts, and the professions. But how does either the verbal formulas "founding peoples" or "nation of immigrants" make a Cree or Mohawk feel?

Most of those who reached these shores likely imagined Canada not in positive terms—a real or a potential Eldorado, Utopia, or City of God in the American style—but negatively as a place they could go to from somewhere worse. Or because they couldn't get into the United States. Has much changed? The media hype for the government policy of multiculturalism plays on the concept of a mosaic: the idea that there can be unity in diversity. Pragmatically, some immigrants welcome multiculturalism: spare cash always comes in handy. A long-resident Serbian librarian once noted that multiculturalism was a relatively inexpensive way of making newcomers feel welcome. Dribbling out a few dollars to dance troupes and folkloric festivals hardly substantiates conservatives' fears that the public is subsidizing terrorist enclaves. On the other hand, is there not an implicit colouration of self-satisfied tokenism?

Mixed feelings inflect our perception of media entertainment, in which multiculturalist tendencies blend with various forms of affirmative action. One sees newspaper and magazine ads and TV commercials showing a massed multi-ethnic sales force of an insurance company or automaker like some big happy dusky family. In TV cop, doctor, or courtroom dramas, or in movie features, minority faces duly appear. If there's a handicapped (read "other-abled") woman-of-colour judge or emergency-room surgeon in play, all the better—such doubling up both testifies to virtue and lowers production costs. Cynicism aside, it's good to see these people, though their presence is heavily weighted toward the urban middle or professional classes, and even at that, misleadingly imply that our society is not white-dominated. Their frequent appearance on the page or screen must seem like a sick joke to a doctor, engineer, or academic from, say, Delhi or Nairobi, who must run a bureaucratic gauntlet in order to get professional accreditation—or employment.

## A Television Triptych

First panel. A friend visiting from Dakka invited my wife and me to join his son-in-law and daughter in celebrating the feast of Id al-Fitr, marking the end of Ramadan. From the small kitchen of the high-rise apartment, the women steadily served us a sequence of savoury dishes. The fact that they would only wait on us, declined to dine with us, aroused what seemed to be unsuspected, or at least long-quiescent, feminist instincts in my wife. More precisely, she resented that her hosts, however kindly their intentions, were imposing on her the status of Honourary Man.

It was cheerful open house as social-call visitors drifted in and out, some of the men taking up living-room stations in front of the big-screen TV. These recently arrived Bangladeshis were intently watching, evidently enjoying, a hockey game. But why would they be watching hockey instead of the familiar soccer or even cricket? Well, why wouldn't they? They were living in Canada, and ice hockey, that combination of ballet and mugging, is our national game.

Second panel. A brightly lit Pakistani place, open long hours for the convenience of hungry cab drivers. Behind the cash register, where a concave oven turns out smoking rotis and parathas with preternatural speed, are a few small tables facing a giant screen. You can spoon your chicken curry while taking in the action. A very beautiful woman in a sari, or sometimes in a tight dress, is very unhappy about something.

Dangerously driven cars come roaring round a bend. A couple of men seem to be having a normal conversation and then one of them pulls out a gun and shoots the other, for no apparent reason. Everyone's speaking Urdu.

Third panel. An East African restaurant. A frugal foodie, I am there for the cheap exotic eats. The worried-looking waiter plunks down a metal plate with beef stew on rice, brings an unasked-for glass of thin orange juice and, even more unexpectedly, tosses me an unpeeled banana. At other little tables, lanky Somali men are staring at the unavoidable screen. Like the Bangladeshis, they're watching a hockey game. Abruptly the channel switches to basketball. This is more explicable. After all, basketball is a game dominated by tall black men. But the dribbling, whirling, leaping only lasts a few moments. Then we are back to hockey.

Perhaps the Bangladeshis' and Somalis' absorbed interest in hockey shouldn't be surprising. If one is interested in sports at all, hockey is a good game to watch. Moreover, immigration, or at least importation, has changed it drastically: in the NHL, or even in junior leagues, Slavic and Scandinavian names abound. More profoundly, this triptych illustrates appositions. With its big-screen Urdu drama, the Pakistani place was engaged in cultural retention; the screens of the Bangladeshi and Somali signalled acculturation. Acculturation may be a soft term for assimilation. On the way to it, the shapes of syncretism suggest that it's possible for the palm to co-exist with the maple.

## A Ballad of Baggage

In September 2001 some friends and I mounted a multimedia show called *A Ballad of Baggage*. It involved slide projections, taped music, a video, and spoken poetry. The proprietor of the art gallery where we staged our show, Nikola Belchevski, was from Macedonia, and the director, the documentary film-maker Antonia Miovska, was an ethnic Macedonian raised in Czechoslovakia. Our group included the poet Goran Simic and the sculptor Aleksandar Bukvic, Bosnian Serbs from besieged Sarajevo, and the photographer Berge Arabian, an Armenian born in Syria. The show's core was a sequence of alternating poems by Simic and myself, a sort of duel. Simic's contributions could be summed up by the title of his 2004 poetry collection, *Immigrant Blues*. Mine were in the voice of an eloquent bigot, who loathes immigrants and immigration. To him, immigrants bring smelly crowds and alien music, jabber unintelligibly, breed indiscriminately, extort pity and handouts from us, steal jobs and send money out of the country, import ancient quarrels and contemporary bombs.

My part of the show brought out contrasting audience reactions. Several native-born liberals squirmed with disquiet. Perhaps labouring under the illusion that poets should express themselves with utter sincerity, they recoiled at my violent abusive language: *Nobody should say these things*. The newcomers to Canada, who in fact made up most of the crowd, instantly grasped what I was doing dramatically. The ironic smiles that crept across their faces seemed to say: *Yes, this is how Canadians see us*.

# Some Lives Are More Important

## ARUN P MUKHERJEE

On the morning of November 9, 1987 just before seven a.m. I climbed down the stairs, still half asleep, and started my day with my usual ritual: I turned on the CBC news. As I filled the kettle to boil water for my tea, the top stories started coming. Bombs had exploded in two parts of the world, one in Colombo, and another in Enniskillen, killing and wounding scores of innocent people. The eighties were a troubled time in both Sri Lanka and Ireland, the LTTE and IRA carrying out bomb attacks in pursuit of their goals.

In those days, my radio stayed on the entire morning tuned to CBC. (Nowadays it is mostly silent.) So it was still on when the eight a.m. news came. To my surprise, the news was different this time. The Colombo story had been dropped. The Enniskillen story had been lengthened. The voice of a grieving father lamented the death of his daughter. A woman mourned her husband.

I learned a harsh truth that day. The lives of the twenty-seven dead and dozens wounded in Sri Lanka were not as important as those of eleven dead and dozens wounded in Ireland. I was angry enough to pull out my telephone book out of the drawer, look up the CBC's number and call. I was so angry that I screamed at the operator who, poor thing, had nothing to do with the news; "Don't people in Colombo mourn too," I demanded.

I have no idea if my concerns were communicated to the newsroom. But my anger that day has remained a very strong memory in my brain. I am not the type of person who calls radio or TV stations and this was the first and last time I did so.

Of course I did not remember the date while writing these words. I had to check the Internet sites to find out when the two cities were bombed on the same day. I did not expect to find the information as quickly as I did. But it is all there, still alive in the hearts and minds of those who were wounded or bereaved that day.

I have often wondered why the CBC dropped one story entirely after the seven a.m. news and "humanized" the other by embellishing it with the voices of the victims. Is it because they had a reporter in Enniskillen who rushed to the scene of the carnage and none in Colombo? Or is it because the Irish are racially and culturally closer to those in the CBC newsroom? It seems to me that the two ideas are connected.

I have also come to realize that there are very different standards in the Canadian media for judging the actions of Western versus non-Western people. So when the mob in Falluja killed four American mercenaries and hung their dismembered bodies on the girders of the Tigris bridge last May, the CBC news opened that night with the description of those acts as "barbaric," "evil," and "brutal," all in one sentence. A couple of sentences later Peter Mansbridge used the word "desecration" to describe the Iraqi mob's actions. The next day, the *Toronto Star* editorial was also studded with such expressions of outrage. However, I have not heard or seen similar words employed in the media to describe the "shock and awe" that was unleashed on the Iraqi people, very ironically, on the eve of the International Day for the Elimination of All Forms of Racism, i.e., March 20, 2003. (I suppose by the time the bombs fell on Baghdad, it was already March 20 there.)

I am sure I am not the only person wondering why the Canadian media were so outraged by the brutality shown by the Iraqi crowd in their killing of four Americans when the brutality that has been perpetrated on Iraq over the last twelve years does not get reported in the same way. I have not seen or heard a single report where the Americans have been called barbaric or savage. But that is what their acts amount to. The successive American governments, with the collusion of other Western governments, have killed at least a million Iraqi men, women, and children since the First Gulf War, either by bombing them from the skies or depriving them of the necessities of life. But this American and British barbarism is not reported in the language of morality and ethics.

Although American, British, and French planes bombed Iraq in daily sorties over the last twelve years, this bombing, and the killing caused by it, was hardly ever in the news. It was completely normalized.

After the start of the Second Gulf War in March 2003, the Western media only showed the bombs lighting up the sky. If Michael Moore's *Fahrenheit 9/11* had such a visceral impact on the audiences, it is because he showed the grief-stricken ordinary Iraqis standing amidst the ruins of their homes, cursing the Americans. The lamentations of Iraqi people have been more or less erased from the North American media. They don't make the news.

But the suffering of American victims of war seems to be always newsworthy. Rosie DiManno of the *Toronto Star* travelled to the States to report on the feelings of the family of Nick Berg, who was beheaded by Iraqi insurgents. The story is emotive and carries a large photograph of Berg's sister "collect[ing] cards from the floral arrangements left at the family home" (A10 May 13, 2004). However, the only places where I can read abut the pain and losses of Iraqis are a few websites run by some very brave and conscientious Americans.

Rosie DiManno was also the *Toronto Star*'s reporter who was sent to Iraq. However, what objectivity or compassion can one expect from someone who wrote a column supporting the war just before it started, opining that she felt that the Americans "did not intervene enough"? I will never forget these words of hers, so shocked I was by the vision of the world encapsulated by them. One would think that such opinions would be considered crassly imperialist and not worthy of a democratic country's citizen. However, such opinions are not that uncommon among the Canadian media people.

*The Globe and Mail* sent Margaret Wente, and I remember being totally numbed by her column, in which she described the gallantry of young US soldiers who arranged a makeshift shower for her and a trip to the Baghdad market, which was bursting with goods. I suppose the bombs that fell during her visit were so well targeted that they fell only on Saddam and his henchmen.

If I don't begin my mornings by reading the daily newspaper or listening to the radio news these days, it is because I need to protect myself from the onslaughts of this asymmetrical valuation of lives.

Just as lives of people in the non-West are less valuable, so, it seems, are their minds. I remember reading a column by Ms Wente where she heaped mountains of contempt on the stupidity of the governments of Namibia and other southern African countries who had refused the free American gift of GM corn. She found it incredible that they refused this food when their populations were starving. Had she bothered to check, it was not that these governments were refusing the gift. What the governments had said was that while they would be grateful to accept ground corn, they could not risk their farmers saving some of this GM corn as seed and ending up contaminating the local varieties. This genuine fear on their part, which has been expressed by many farming communities around the world, obviously had no resonance for Ms Wente. For her these countries were beggars with an attitude and no more.

I am not a media expert and what I am writing about is based on my responses to the rivers of news and comment that pass by me every day. I am only writing about some of the most painful stories that stayed in my mind. I would love to write about many of the clippings in my files about reports that downplay Canadian mining companies' poor environmental practices that have killed river life and deprived people of drinking water, as in Guyana in 1996 and the Philippines in 2004, but that would require a lengthy linguistic analysis of many stories.

Generally speaking, I am not the addressee of the Canadian media's discourse. The "we" they use excludes my feelings and my affiliations in the world. I am, for example, deeply troubled by how the people of Diego Garcia were forcibly evacuated from their country thirty years ago and dumped in Mauritius. The British then leased this island to the United States to make a naval base. It is from this base in the Indian Ocean that the American planes took off, with bombs that were dropped on Iraq.

The thousands of displaced Diego Garcians were given only seven million dollars collectively as compensation. They still live in dire poverty in slums in Mauritius. While the US navy lures its recruits by describing the natural beauty of the island and its beaches and sports facilities, the British have passed an order in council taking away the right of abode of the people of Diego Garcia.

My Internet search for coverage of this story in the Canadian media brought up zero results. I cannot but conclude that the Canadian media is not interested in stories of Western imperialist powers' unjust treatment of non-Western people. Their suffering will not be made present to the Canadian consciousness.

On the other hand, the winner of *Jeopardy* made prime time news last night on several radio and TV stations.

My overwhelming feeling when reading a Canadian newspaper or watching a Canadian television programme is that of an outsider. The talking heads or columnists are uniformly white, barring a very few exceptions. The choice of news stories and the slant used is heavily determined by their whiteness. The Canadian media have very few correspondents stationed in non-Western countries. So, one Asia bureau correspondent might travel around and gain instant expertise on this massive continent.

The stories filed by these instant experts, or the columnists at home writing with authority about the world from within their self-righteous viewpoints come across to me, and many others like me, as disrespectful of non-Western people's humanity. Media analysis is a very difficult process and Noam Chomsky's painstaking and detailed studies are daunting in their very massiveness. As an ordinary reader and viewer, what I have attempted here is to communicate my pain and anger when I read about, hear, and see the world refracted through the mind of white Canadian journalists.

# Reflections on a Black Radio Station and the National Broadcaster

## Cecil A Foster

## Introduction

During the decade of the 1990s, I was involved in a supporting role in what we presented then as a struggle by a group of financiers within the Black community in the Toronto area for an urban/Black radio station. My primary contribution was as a journalist, columnist, and radio talk-show host. In the main, my argument, with all its idealism, was that Blacks in Canada's largest city needed a radio station as a sign of recognition that they belonged in Canada. As I presented it, and as I understood the financiers' arguments that I at times parroted, the struggle for a Black radio station was a major test of multiculturalism and liberal democracy in Canada. It was a struggle for recognition and authentic representation by a group of Canadians that historically had been marginalized in society. Black Canadians, the main argument went, needed outlets in the media that presented positive images of them in all their humanity and differences. They also needed positions and platforms of articulation from within the media that allowed them to help shape the dominant culture. Indeed, the financiers went a step further: they argued that because Blacks in the Toronto area were a distinct community they needed a radio station to cater exclusively to their needs and aspirations.

As I now write, there has been a Black/urban radio station in Toronto for three years, but somehow it is nothing like what I had imagined or even hoped it would be. The programming is not what I had anticipated or even what I recalled hearing the financiers promising the Black community in the Toronto area in return for its support during the crucial struggle to get the radio licence. When I talk to people in the Black community—including many who were in the vanguard of the struggle for a Black radio station—they too seem disappointed. With the exception of those a generation or so younger than me, fewer of them even listen to the station. Indeed, the programming seems to assume that they would not be among the listenership. The Black/urban radio is not for them and it does not really want them as listeners.

Instead, these old warriors have reverted to old listening habits, relying on the national broadcaster for their primary source of information and entertainment by radio. This, even though they acknowledge that there are still significant gaps in the way the Canadian Broadcasting Corporation continues to present and represent the Canadian Black experience. We have returned to, or stayed with, by and large, a CBC Radio that we had offered up as the best excuse for why Canada, in general, and Toronto, in the specific, needed a Black radio station. Contradictions, and ironies, indeed.

What would account for this "alienation" when I listen to the Black radio station, and why is it that I still find CBC Radio more "authentic"—positions that are contrary to what I, and presumably thousands of other Blacks in the Toronto area, expected?

How we answer these questions might depend on whether we still hold the idealistic position that it is possible for a single radio station to bring recognition and harmony to a community as diverse internally as is the Black community of Toronto and surrounding areas. It depends on whether we subscribe to the idea of self-sufficient monadic cultures within multiculturalism. It also matters whether we think that realistic, as opposed to idealistic, forms of representation and recognition should come through a relationship with similarly situated and even equal groups within the same universe. Should recognition and representation be viewed through inclusive lenses, or should they be seen as strengthened by and dependent on exclusion—wrapping any ethnic or racialized group in its own culture and setting it adrift from all others? More than that, the answer would also depend on what role we see a Black/urban radio station playing within the so-called Black community and within the wider society that is multicultural Canada. And just as important, the answer might very well depend on whether we think there is, indeed, an entity in Canada called the Black community and if there is such a community is there any unit to it.

My position in this analysis is that, in hindsight, it was inevitable that there be contradictions between what was championed as the role for a Black and urban station and what is being delivered in terms of programming, audience concentration, and the changing motives behind the "need" for such a radio station. Indeed, on reflection, it can be argued that it was inevitable that the radio station would become the site of a Hegelian unhappy consciousness—where despite the best of intentions on the part of everyone involved, nobody seemed to be very happy with the outcome. In this regard, what happened to the Black community in Toronto and "its" radio station is a smaller version of the contradictions and unhappiness that seem to be endemic to multiculturalism in general, and specifically to the role and positioning of the media in a multicultural Canada. It is for this reason, for good or ill, that multiculturalism in Canada means that we seem to be fated to live always in a state where none of us is ever totally happy with the way things are, but at the same time we recognize that things would be worse off if they were not the way they are.

## The Media and Their Role

The most common definition of the media is that it is the collective or plural of the term or concept *medium,* in the sense that a newspaper is a medium of communication, as is a radio station, a magazine, a television station, a billboard, a newsletter and any other method that we use to exchange information. Bringing all these methods of communicating together creates a plural body that is the media. Making them as widely available as possible to a population makes them broadcast, as opposed to narrowcast or restricted, media. Allowing members of society to own them makes the media public, as opposed to being held privately by the government on behalf of the public. The government-owned Canadian Broadcasting Corporation radio and television services as well as those educational media services owned by various provinces, however, operate under mandates that require them to act in many cases as if they were owned by public individuals.

The operative definition that I want to suggest for this analysis is that we think of media as deriving from the word to mediate. This means that there are at least two or more entities that are involved in a dialectical relationship: mediate means a way of trying to produce a reconciliation of positions, so that they can be contained within a wider body. In this case, the wider body is a multicultural Canada where there can be several dialectical and oppositional forces, views or positions within the body politick. I am relying on the old philosophical notion that to mediate implies a sense of having relations and an intention to come to a reconciliation of positions. The actors in the negotiations are acting in good faith and have intentions that are good, for what is generally called the societally or culturally common good. They are not by intention evil.

Everything that occurs, even when it appears as new or as *news,* flows out of some previous occurrence, event, or thought. In many respects, what is thought and the actions that we take flow out of reception or received knowledge—information and a way of knowing that is subjective and steeped in what our culture hands to us. It is, therefore, related to something that went before it and most likely to events and occasions that will follow. This might put us into the area of causes and effects, but for this moment it might be sufficient to say that the media are really about how we develop, structure, and maintain relationships within a culture and society.

What this way of seeing and knowing does is to place us in the position where context is always important. Therefore, how we are situated in, or embedded in, a wider society or narrower ethnic or racialized community helps to set the stage for how we are mediated in the media.

Out of the context arise the various contradictions and ironies of individual cases that are part of a wider unity that is the overall context or
universal position that is multicultural Canada. The context also
involves being situated in a specific or particular community: in this
case, a so-called Black community that is just one ethnicized or racialized grouping within the universal that is Canada.

Therefore, we may want to keep before us the seeming contradiction: that a Black/urban station that resulted from a community struggle for a Black/urban station might not reflect the Black community as
some of us imagined. Furthermore, there would be the seeming contradiction that the recognition that some of us might have wanted might
have to come from the very source that we rejected and which was oppositional to the idea of a Black radio station—that being the more universalizing CBC Radio that hopes to reflect the particularizing identities of all members of the universal that is multicultural Canada.

There is, as well, a second sense of media that I want us to consider. This emanates from what I have just described, but in a way that
gives the institutions and agencies that we now call the media an active
role in society. We need to recognize the media as active social agents.
This is where we may think of them as mediators—those agents either
as individuals or institutions that act as go-between for two or more different sides. Their job is to produce a compromise—a new position—
that is a reconciliation of all the old positions held by the parties in the
mediation. Our hope is that as mediators they strive objectivity and are
of an independent view and disposition. Their role is to carry and bring
news to and from the different parties, and this could be very central to
their role, to elucidate and even to teach one party about the good and
evils of the other party's position.

In this case, the mediator has an active and important role that helps
all the parties to determine what is good for them and to arrive at a higher understanding and an agreement about the common good. An important element of this job is that of explaining and evaluating what is presented as new or news. This evaluation can only be meaningful if the
mediator can relate the new or news to the parties seeking reconciliation—therefore the mediator must be understanding and even representative, authentically, of both positions at the same time. Not demonstrat-
ing this authenticity, genuineness, and familiarity with the arguments

and positions of all sides involved in the reconciliation effort would make the mediation ineffective and even leave the mediator open to charges of not acting in good faith or of favouring one or more sides. In such a case, the credibility of the mediator would be at stake.

In our particular case of an urban or Black radio station, it is important when a radio station that is supposedly Black and urban puts specific images of what is culturally Black and urban on the air. Just as important, symbolically and representationally, is what such a radio station leaves out or does not elevate as representational of what is Black and urban. Once again, we may be left with the contradiction of turning to a universalizing medium like CBC Radio to reflect the particulars of a representational group within the wider body politick. This might be the case, for example, when CBC deems it fit to seek out Black and urban voices to speak on political issues, whereas a supposedly Black and urban station might be silent by not providing a forum for any real political debate. Indeed, in this case we can see a wider "mediating" role for a CBC Radio by holding in tension the different views and positions common among different groups within the universal culture. The overriding culture becomes the site for the different views emanating from perspectives and perceptions that need to be placed in dialectical opposition. The result is theoretically a higher meaning and new knowledge within the existing universal culture, and the recognition of the particular ethnic group within the wider universal, Canada.

## Media Perspective

As a long-time news hand myself, I am familiar with an old refrain that people in the business like to repeat as frequently as possible: the nature of news-gathering is like an incurable disease or your very first love. Once you become smitten by it, the newshounds like to say, you can never get it out of your system. Once acquired, as the traditional wisdom goes, you can never lose your nose for news or your interest in wanting to know what is going on not only in your neighbourhood, but in all those far off places that you may never visit. More than that, there will always be that hunger to tell someone what you know, to add to other people's storehouse of knowledge about what is good and evil, or to ask those purportedly tough questions that any other person in your position would be asking—all in the service of a free and unrestricted flow of information on which knowledge can be based and updated.

Once a reporter, editor, columnist, or newscaster, at heart you will always be one, even when the end has come, when someone writes thirty in brackets to finish what is the story of your personal odyssey, or when, supposedly, everything fades personally and finally to black. Even then, a reporter will still be a reporter. His or her essence would remain. There is another side to this story and it is that people in general cannot "get it," neither can they really understand what is so enigmatic about journalism, if they have never been touched by this seeming disease that transfigures otherwise normal citizens into "ink strained wrenches" or to have news or ink flowing in their veins. News, therefore, is something that you just have to know, and everybody doesn't. Once a person becomes a journalist, the mythology of the industry goes, she or he becomes unchangeably a news person. They can never become, genuinely, something else, even if they were to leave the profession.

This notion of an unchanging nose for news is presented generally as a good thing. A nose for news ultimately improves society and helps us all to make decisions that produce the most good for all of us. A nose for news supposedly equips the news gatherer or presenter with an eternal curiosity and causes her or him to be constantly on the lookout for what is new. Even if a nose for news is seemingly unchanging, what it detects is change. It is always searching out and identifying what is new, what has changed from a previous state so that it has become new. Idealistically, this is what, as a commodity, news is: all that is new in terms of what has not happened before, what has changed into a news state or status, and what was not generally anticipated. Added to that, news is generally presented as all those developments that really matter to the consumer in a direct way—where the acquisition of what is new in her or his immediate environment contributes to making the consumer a more informed citizen and a rational being who can digest bits of information and make rational and good decisions based on the merit of this news. Therefore, news supposedly tells us what has changed or is changing and as rational beings we take this knowledge and determine how we will handle, perhaps even control, the changes.

A nose for news means, significantly, that at a higher level of knowing, much of what journalists do is really instinctual—often they do it without exactly knowing why. In this sense, by relying on a nose for news, they are creatures of their cultures, somewhat akin to robots performing according to the way they are programmed. A nose for news allows the newshound to recognize certain signals or symbols and to deduce what is new or news.

What is new or news gets placed in relationship to being compared or contrasted to what was not new, to what was supposedly unchangeable, or to what has become something other than what it was previously. News is based on expectations, for they are descriptions of probabilities. What makes what is new news is the social value that we place on the newness and on the likelihood of an occurrence or nonoccurrence This social value comes out of our culture, our perception and perspective of what is good and evil, what is changeable and unchangeable, and what would be to the benefit of society if descriptions and explanations of what has occurred are widespread. For, indeed, everything that is new is not news—because in making judgements of what is good or ill for society, what has occurred, or not occurred, is maybe viewed as insignificant. The very value of whether something is newsworthy means that the information about it comes to us already mediated: someone, or some agency or institution that knows our culture and knows what is good or evil in general makes a determination of what is news and what would be in our best interest to know.

The arguments for having a radio station with an ethnicized and racialized Black focus were made along the lines that we have just examined, probing the roles of the media and the kinds of perspectives and points of view that journalists and radio personalities have. An argument was made that Canadian Blacks needed a forum through which they could mediate the news and information that was presented to the wider community, and even to Blacks themselves, about them. In this regard, the argument ran, only Blacks really knew their essences, for only Blacks would really know what was changeable and unchangeable about them. A similar argument was that Black Canadians needed a forum that effectively validated their way of life as "nothing new" or dangerous. Idealistically, this would be a medium to explain to the wider society that Black cultural life has been for a long time a significant component of the unchangeable multicultural culture and ethnicity that is Canada.

To this end, the proposed radio station would be as subjective as any other while aiming for objectivity as an ideal. Its subjectivity would be towards the supposedly Black community, rather than against the Black community, as was generally accepted by that community to be the case with most mainstream media. A Black radio station, speaking on behalf of the community, would help to determine what was important to members of the community, and be able to bring unity to the community out of its diversity and differences. A Black radio station, finally, would show that members of the Black community had the financial and business acumen to run a radio profitably.

## Caribana, Hurricane Reports, and Cricket Scores

I was out for a drive in Ontario in the summer of 2004 on the Saturday of the long weekend that marks what is now called Caribana Weekend. I knew that people from all over the world had been descending in large numbers on Toronto for well over a week. In a sense, there was nothing new about the throngs of people that were in Toronto for the festival, the highlight of which was the annual street parade on the Saturday of the long weekend. Such crowds had become routine since Caribana started as a festival in 1967. For years, the organizers of Caribana had battled municipal, provincial, and federal authorities for recognition of the festival as important not only to the civic pride of southern Ontario, but to the economy of Canada and to the country's image as a teeming multicultural mosaic. In what now seems to be a struggle in ancient times, back then, Caribana officials had a hard time arguing with representatives of the three levels of government that the festival was an important economic generator and was therefore worthy of the taxpayers' support through subsidies and grants from various levels of government.

Full official recognition came to Caribana in the summer of 2003, a year in Canada's and Toronto's history that is noted for what is now known as the Severe Acute Respiratory Syndrome (SARS) crisis that for a while put the entire tourist industry in Canada in its sick bed. With people the world over staying away from Toronto, in the specific, and Canada, in general, authorities at all levels decided to dig deep into their pockets and to offer a life line to the various cultural events that were suffering because of the fear of SARS, but which when revived could be used as the agents to help resuscitate the national tourism industry. Caribana was one of the festivals to be placed on the list of major national events that underpin the national and regional economy and the entire country's sense of itself as a multicultural body. Caribana had officially moved from a position where it was seen as antagonistic to the common good to a new position where it was seen as indispensable to the economic and common good of not only Toronto and Southern Ontario, but also the country as a whole.

So, while driving along, I had the car radio on an all-news radio station. At the top of the hour came a report by one of those perky young female reporters, telling the world that one million visitors were on the streets of Toronto celebrating Caribana. Oh, how times have changed, I thought: once, Caribana officials were sneered at when they said that the entire festival attracted a total of one million people, including visitors and residents, to the festival over a three-day period. I remembered writing in the mainstream media and discussing on talk radio the size of the draw that was Caribbean and of the times when officials within the various levels of government, Metro Toronto Police, Metro Toronto Convention Centre, and the association representing the Toronto area hoteliers and restaurateurs had pooh-poohed the one-million figure for the festival. (For a detailed discussion of this debate, see Foster's *A Place Called Heaven: The Meaning of Being Black In Canada).*

Back then, Caribana's own claim of one million people was based on visitors and Toronto residents attending the festival. Now, according to this reporter, Caribana was attracting one million visitors to the parade alone, and nobody was even querying these numbers. This was the 37th annual parade, the report said. Then came the sign-off and the shocker for me as a Canadian and an old newshand: the reporter announcing in her breathless upbeat way that she was reporting from her very first attendance at a Caribana Parade. Indeed, it is still possible for news reporters at major radio stations never to have visited a Caribana parade, even when the festival is almost forty years old. Obviously, then, Caribana was not as important to the image of Canada as was being claimed; either that or it was still possible for young boys and girls to grow into socially developed men and women without experiencing what is considered to be the greatest outdoors festival in Canada, and which, as this reporter noted, was attracting visitors from around the world. More important, obviously, reporters can still become one-day experts when forced to report on the exotic, as opposed to speaking with authority because of familiarity with what is being reported upon and from a position of cultural embeddedness.

But, to some extent, in an idealized world what the all-news radio was telling me, a Black man living in Southern Ontario, about Caribana should not have really mattered. I should have been getting knowledgeable information from reporters on a Black/urban station who could speak with the authority and subjectivity that this report could not. Indeed, there was a Black and urban station. Except for a few cursory mentions of Caribana, the festival may as well be happening in another town and community worlds away, rather than right in the heart of the community that the Black/urban stations was supposed to represent. And what was true for Caribana, was also true for news from Africa and the Caribbean.

Hurricanes were annually wreaking havoc on Caribbean islands, but anyone expecting a careful and understanding explanation of what was happening would find only silence on Toronto's Black/urban station. The same was true for scores and commentaries when West Indian cricket teams took on the world, most notably South Africa, part of the continent that supporters of the Black/urban station had promised would be high on their priority list. Indeed, festivals and events at home and abroad in parts of the "Black" world were noted for their absented presences on this station that was supposed to place Toronto and its doings within a Black world, and to speak of them with caring, knowledge, and authority. In many respect, the reports on the Black/urban station were often more superficial in details and understanding of the local environment than what could be found elsewhere on the radio dial—notably on CBC Radio. This was not what had been promised.

## A Black Radio Station: The Promise

A Black radio station, proponents had argued, would not only speak with authority about Black Canadians to all Canadians, but also give Black Canadians a notable voice in the all-important social, political, and cultural debates of the day. A Black radio station would be an act of participatory democracy, or so I and others had argued. The simple act of owning a radio station would be a powerful commentary that, symbolically, Black Canadians belonged in this country, especially among those who were entrusted with the care and protection of one of the prize possessions of the nation-state—its airwaves.

A high point of this struggle was when the Black financiers, now called Milestone Radio Inc., locked horns with the Canadian Broadcasting Corporation over who should operate on what is perhaps the strongest signal on the FM band in the greater Toronto Area. Milestone argued before the regulatory Canadian Radio-television and Telecommunications Commission (CRTC) that it was "entitled" to a radio station and to the 99.1 spot on the FM dial. Its argument was straightforward: hundreds of thousands of Blacks in the Greater Toronto area did not have a radio station that appealed to them. The prevailing fare on radio, which included CBC Radio Toronto that was then operating on the AM dial, did not reflect the tastes of Blacks in the region. What was offered, they argued, and this became the refrain that I helped carry to the wider media, did not come with a Black signature.

Milestone argued that anyone wanting to hear reggae and calypso music or any other Caribbean tempo had to wait until the few community radio stations around Toronto provided an hour or so of Caribbean programming. Often this meant waiting until the multilingual Toronto Radio Station CHIN-FM provided Caribbean programming late on Saturday nights or when the university community radio stations provided an hour or two of Caribbean programming every week. This was not good enough, Milestone argued. It would integrate music from around the world into its regular programming, so that it would be routine on the morning show, the afternoon show, and the drive home show to hear African and Caribbean vibes and rhythms that were seldom—indeed, never, it argued—heard on Canadian regular radio.

And, Milestone argued, there was seldom any news about sports and politics that were of interest to Black Canadians, especially news about cricket and soccer. Similarly, there was no news about what was happening in Africa and the Caribbean, and no real news on what was the Black experience within Canada, in general, and the Great Toronto Area, in the specific. Indeed, there was no integrated programming offering Blacks the "oldies but goldies" music of bygone eras, such as Motown.

If Toronto Area Blacks wanted to hear such music—which Milestone said it knew from its polling that Blacks wanted to hear—then listeners had to turn to WBLK in Buffalo, a radio station that for advertising purposes had adopted Blacks in the Toronto area. Milestone argued that it would repatriate those Canadian listeners and keep the money for advertising and sponsorship in Canadian pockets. It would do the job that CBC and other radio stations were failing to do, even though meeting the needs of all Canadians was part of the national broadcaster's mandate. Milestone would give Blacks a place on the radio. Milestone would do for Black Canadians what the national broadcaster could not, or would not: it would give them a voice and speak to a meaningful presence.

Milestone did lose its bid for the 99.1 FM spot, with the CRTC obviously accepting the argument by the CBC that the national broadcaster should have the strongest signal because it, effectively, represented all Canadians. Indeed, on its webpage, Milestone now recalls the struggle and disappointment it suffered during its first official efforts in 1990 to get a radio licence. Getting the licence was an act of advocacy, as the group relied on strong community support and political intervention to bolster its plans. Such was the case, in the struggle with CBC. Indeed, this is the narrative of a community-backed struggle that led to the establishment of the first Black or urban radio station in Canada, as told by Milestone Radio Inc. on its official web page. Milestone's statement is worth quoting at length:[1]

> Bolstered by the positive results of the study, the mid-90s were a time of rebuilding as Milestone began to prepare for its second bid for a CRTC licence. In its second application, Milestone once again received widespread support with an unprecedented 12,000 letters of intervention written in support of the company. To the disappointment of Milestone's many supporters, the CRTC voted to award the licence to the CBC by a controversial 3-2 majority.

I used my position within the media to criticize CBC for muscling out Milestone and CRTC for not being sensitive enough to the needs of the Black community. I used my position to argue for a Black radio station. The next time a spot became available on the FM dial, Milestone was in a better position influentially and strategically. It had significant segments of the Black community behind it, and it had political good-will from all those in authority who believed that not only had Milestone been rejected when the CRTC heard earlier applications, but also, that it was the Black community had been shut out. As Milestone states:

> Milestone appealed the decision and followed with a powerful public campaign to petition the Federal Cabinet. Milestone addressed the Council of City of Scarborough regarding the appeal and was awarded a favourable vote. Similar resolutions were subsequently submitted by the City of York and the City of Toronto on behalf of the group.
>
> In May 1998, in response to Milestone's appeal, the Federal Cabinet sent the CRTC an Order in Council to reserve a frequency on the FM band for applicants bearing in mind Toronto's diverse society and the need for employment equity. Several months later the CRTC announced that it would once again call for applications for Toronto radio service. In the following year Milestone readied its application for the frequency of 93.5 on the FM dial. The new application again received widespread support and gained even further credibility when Standard Broadcasting became a minority investor in the station.

Milestone, eventually, received permission to start a Black/urban radio station, and Flow 93.5FM started broadcasting February 6, 2001—going on air pointedly in a month that is now generally associated with Black culture and belonging and is generally known as Black History Month. There was much joy and fanfare in the Toronto Black community. I was happy, even though I was not one of the financiers, that I had played a role in presenting the argument for the radio station in columns I was writing for the *Toronto Star*, in a strategically placed feature in the *Ottawa Citizen* to catch the eyes of the federal politicians and bureaucrats, and on a talk-show named *Urban Talk* on the Toronto radio station CFRB 1010AM, the flagship of the Standard Broadcasting Corp. Like many of my friends, and others in my age group, I looked forward to having a radio station that "included" me demographically.

The disappointment for me was almost immediate. The new station, dubbed Flow 93.5FM, is on the air and apparently growing in strength. When I ask my children how Flow is doing they all agree that it is *wicked,* which means that, at least for them, it is doing really well. Milestone has described its format and programming this way:

Within the present radio and music industries, Urban refers to a diverse, cosmopolitan music format based on Rhythm and Blues music and related genres. This format is a modern-day reflection of the rich musical traditions of Black musicians and Black-influenced music over the past century.

What we call Urban today is a mosaic reflecting the contribution of a varied group of artists over the last four decades. In the 50s the sound was defined by artists such as Chuck Berry, Little Richard and Sam Cooke. In the following decade artists such as James Brown, Aretha Franklin and Otis Redding helped shape the sound. During the 70s, it was Stevie Wonder, Marvin Gaye and Bob Marley. The 80s featured George Clinton, Michael Jackson and Run DMC with Janet Jackson and Whitney Houston emerging in the early 90s. Today such well-known artists as 50 Cent, Beyonce, Glenn Lewis and Jully Black are making their own contribution to this popular sound.

But has Flow 93.5FM really brought the programming, the inclusiveness for Blacks, and the recognition that its financiers had promised? What is still not on the air is the programming that had been promised. Still not heard on a regular and consistent basis, which means integrated into normal programming, are most of the artists mentioned in the radio's blurb on what is urban music. Still no cricket or soccer scores or commentaries; no reports on politics and social affairs in Africa and the Caribbean; no substantive debates on issue facing the Black community in Canada and the Greater Toronto Area; no regular and integrated reggae, calypso, soca or hi-life music in the programming. However, there is plenty of hip-hop music, and virtually no Motown, blues, jazz, and gospel. Indeed, with Flow 93.5FM on the air, some elements of the Black community in Toronto seem to be worse off in terms of choices: to accommodate the new Toronto Black radio station, the signals for WBLK, the Black radio station from Buffalo that was the voice of Blackness and the urban for many Black immigrants and residents in the Toronto area, were blocked out in the greater Toronto area.

Fortunately, for many of the deprived Blacks in the Greater Toronto Area there was still CBC Radio. At least, there is good programming that includes blues, jazz, gospel and even cricket scores in the morning. In addition, there is room now for Black spoken word, for explaining hip-hop and performance poetry, and how this form of entertainment is fusing with expressions from other ethnic groups in Canada. Or, the deprived and rejected among us remained with the community radio stations with their blocks of Black programming at seemingly ungodly hours, which Milestone had criticized and had promised to change if and when it got a licence. Indeed, now that we have a Black/urban radio station, significant segments of the Black community in Toronto need the national broadcaster more than ever. For in the radio station that claims to be Black and urban there is much that large segments of the Black community do not recognize as Black. There is a lot that the community presents as Black and urban that do not have a voice on this station. Indeed, there are many lessons for the learning here. Some of them call for us to honestly reassess the role of the media and even our expectations of the media in Canada.

## A Black Radio Station: A Reality

There are those who would argue that the outcome was inevitable: that in the end Flow 93.5FM has to be a business and that to do so it can not be all things to all people. Indeed, the argument might be made that the owners of the radio station must discriminate even within the so-called Black community and that they choose to offer programming that is more favourable to young urban Blacks and those from other ethnic groups who share their popular music and culture. And the argument might be made that in making their argument for a Black radio station, and in seeking the active support of a community as diverse and different as that in the greater Toronto area, Milestone oversold what it was capable of doing.

Others may argue that this is the price that Milestone, as a group of neophytes in the business world of broadcasting, had to pay as the entry price into the business. Still others have wondered if Milestone could reasonably be expected to maintain the fidelity to its promises to the Black Community when the financiers are now joined in their boardroom by a shareholder from outside the community, who may not share its sensibilities and sensitivities.

Still, all excuses aside, there is still a sadness for many who consider themselves to be part of Black community. This sadness occurs when they happen upon Flow 93.5FM on the dial or on the internet and see and hear in the station more of what it is not than what it is. Indeed, dreams do die hard, and some of them never do. Using hindsight, it is possible to argue cogently that the disappointment that some feel over Flow 93.5FM in Toronto is matched by the joy that much of the younger generation now feel the disappointment they would have felt had the radio station started with some other format.

## Conclusion

There is a wider argument for inclusion that underpins this experience or *news* in Toronto. I want to suggest that the experience with Flow 93.5FM in Toronto shows the possible results of living in an officially multicultural society, but one in which the needs of some ethnicized and racialized groups are approached specifically from a group perspective. Often the solution is presented as that of a particular group withdrawing into and unto itself. Withdrawal is advocated as a way of avoiding contradictions and tensions that stem from having to deal with a multiplicity of other groups. Indeed, this kind of social withdrawal was very much part of the argument initially advanced for a Black radio station as an expression of a specific community's presence and wellbeing in Canada.

In this light, the Black/urban station in Toronto was bound to disappoint, for it is not possible for one radio station to cater effectively to all the needs of any community. This is especially the case for a community as diverse as the Black community in Toronto, an entity that is socially constructed out of people from many cultures and nationalities around the world. Such an observation is contrary to the argument some Black Canadians have tried to make in attempting to move their loyalty away from the national broadcaster towards a more exclusive station. And what we now know as the experience of a Black focus radio station could very well be the same unhappiness that awaits all those advocating for Black focus schools as yet another way of achieving Black recognition, respect, and academic success. (Foster, 1996)

We should remember that what is common about members of this so-called Black community in Canada is that they share superficial characteristics. This determining factor is the colour of their skin or having an ancestry, no matter how remote, that can be traced back to Africa. Substantially, this Black community is itself a multicultural and multi-ethnic being. Its formation is not an act of nature, but of the social will to be included in such a grouping. There is, therefore, very little that is actually unchangeable and unmediated about the so-called Black community. What can be said about the naturalness of the Black community can be extrapolated at a more universal level to represent multicultural Canada. This means that there would be tensions and contradictions within the community, with some of them seemingly beyond reconciliation.

Indeed, if there is such a thing as a Black community, it comes more out of a supposedly shared living experience. To expect a single radio station to cater to all the needs of such a community would be no different than what, in effect, we expected of CBC Radio in multicultural Canada. One of the major differences here is that CBC Radio is fully supported by the public, while a radio station like Flow 93.5FM is not. Therefore, CBC is forced to make some choices and compromises in programming in terms of who it should include and who it should exclude that a profit-driven station like Flow does not have to make.

So why have so many of us returned to CBC Radio? Indeed, it is worth noting that the CBC Radio Toronto Morning show is, at the time of writing, the most popular in the area, something that, ironically, did not happen until there was supposedly greater choice in the Toronto radio market. While I am not suggesting that this dominant position is attributed directly to the presence of Flow 93.5FM in the market, it is true that the presence of this urban station did have at least an indirect effect. For one thing, CBC Radio is now more inclusive of minority and Black groups in terms of what it presents as news and information and in terms of those who do the presenting and the scripting. The compromise in programming at CBC seems to be based on the goal of always striving for greater inclusiveness, the idea that, idealistically, it is better to give as strong a voice as possible to more groups. This is when CBC recognizes that what makes all of us Canadians is the experience of daily living together with one another, with all the tensions and differences that are involved. This is where CBC realizes that Canada is what we imagine it to be and that it is constructed equally out of the lived experiences of all people and groups calling themselves Canadians.

However, this does not always cast CBC in a good light, for there are times when there appears to be no diversity when CBC Radio is dealing with what might be deemed serious and important issues and events. One such event, for example, was the federal elections in 2004, when most of the commentaries and reports were from the usual people and groups that tend to reflect Canada as the two solitudes of old—a Canada that is misconstrued as primarily French and English, or a country in which major decisions are still made within bicultural rather than multicultural sensibilities.

Indeed, perhaps CBC is now perceptually performing much closer to what is required of a national broadcaster—which means that it takes an overall, universal picture of the country and it situates different groups, often in tension and contradictorily, within this bigger universe. The new image of CBC is of one that is coming to terms with the idea that its role is to "mediate" Canada and things Canadian in the widest sense possible, and that where possible it should always be striving for new voices, for more inclusivity in the way it explains Canada and Canadians.

Which, with the use of hindsight, takes us back to that "struggle" in the mid 1990's when CBC Radio Toronto and Milestone were in competition for the strongest signal on the FM dial. Back then I felt strongly that the CRTC made the wrong decision by favouring CBC. Looking back, and now knowing what I know, I have changed that opinion. The CRTC was right to give the strongest signal to the station that represents multicultural Canada as a universal and to give a weaker signal to a station that at best, and even with the best of intentions, caters to only a very small segment of any community at any time. For one of the lessons the experience with the Black/urban radio stations has taught us is that recognition, and some degree of happiness, are best achieved through mediation and that the news about us Canadians is that there is very little about us that is really unchangeable.

## Note

[1] Milestone Radio, Flow 93.5 Urban Flow Case, http://www.milestoneradio.com, (accessed September 6, 2004).

## References

Foster, Cecil. *A Place Called Heaven: The Meaning of Being Black In Canada*. Toronto: HarperCollins Publishers, 1996.

Foster, C. and C. Schwartz. *CARIBANA: The Greatest Celebration*. Toronto: One World Books, 1995.

Hall, Stuart. "Cultural Identity and Diaspora." In *Identity: Community, Culture, Difference*, Jonathan Rutherford. 222-237. London: Lawrence & Wishart, 1990.

————, ed. 1997. Reprint. *Representation: Cultural Representations and Signifying Practices*. London: Sage Publications, 2003.

Taylor, Charles. *Hegel and Modern Society*. Cambridge: Cambridge University Press, 1979.

Milestone Radio, *Flow 93.5*: Urban Flow Case, http://www.milestoneradio.com

# A Happy Compromise:
# Hate Crime Reporting in the
# Toronto *Globe and Mail*

## Michael Neumann

The *Globe and Mail* is a respectable paper. It's probably the most respectable paper in Canada. What's more, it's not owned by hard-line Zionists; Toronto has Izzy Asper's *National Post* to fill that slot. The editor is Jewish, but so what? So am I. Nothing suggests that the *Globe and Mail* ought to be biased in favor of Jews or against Muslims, blacks, and native people.

The *Globe and Mail* abhors racism. The *Globe and Mail* has often condemned racism. But the *Globe and Mail* is racist in one precisely definable sense: it assigns more value to Jews than to other ethnic groups.

The mental processes which generate this assignment are unknown to me. One thing is clear: the *Globe and Mail* folks have a problem.

# A Happy Compromise

They quite sincerely abhor racism yet exhibit a form of it, a classic example of what is known as cognitive dissonance: they have conflicting attitudes which, unmanipulated, would produce considerable discomfort. Fortunately for the *Globe and Mail*, there has emerged a happy compromise.

Its reporters, columnists, and in some cases its sources say all the right things, and cover hate crimes against all ethnic groups. *Globe* articles consistently refer to non-Jewish victims of discrimination with the utmost sympathy and respect—well, as we'll see, usually. The reports convey, more or less, the message that all hate crimes are abhorrent, all are equally important. But—and here is the compromise—newspapers express and convey their values more in the extent of their coverage than in its contents. The *New York Times* could proclaim, when it ran the occasional page 10, 125-word item on irritable bowel syndrome, that irritable bowel syndrome was the most urgent problem confronting the human race. But if cancer grabbed all the front-page coverage, we would understand that the *Times* did not really regard irritable bowel syndrome as a big deal. The fine words would be a lie or an exercise in self-deception. Cancer would have been assigned far more importance. And in its coverage—usually despite its fine words—the *Globe and Mail* conveys just that message about hate crimes against Jews and other ethnic groups: the former are important, the latter are not.

Recently this has become obvious. On March 16, 2004, Jewish homes were spray-painted with slogans. You had to notice because the *Globe and Mail* put the story on about a third of page one, with a photo taking up over half the space above the fold. The story continued on page 8, where it was tastefully paired with two articles on possible anti-semitism at a Toronto golf club. These occupied the entire print area of page 9. The letters column on page 12 led off with two submissions suggesting people needed to pay more attention to antisemitism.

On March 25, an Islamic centre in the Toronto area was spray-painted with slogans and set on fire. Tables were destroyed and chairs thrown outside. The story (March 26) made the bottom of page 12. (The top contained a much longer story, with photograph, about a hairdresser who'd won an African-Canadian Achievement Award.) It got little more space than the page 8 continuation of the March 17 anti-semitism story, and ended—as if to validate the seriousness of the incident—with

63

a statement of solidarity from the Canadian Jewish Congress.

A letter to the *Globe and Mail* about its coverage got no response. Then, a few days later, all hell broke loose.

I am not referring to the start of the Shia revolt in Iraq, which made the front page of the *Globe* on April 6. That story was utterly dwarfed by another: at 2:30 a.m., the United Talmud Torah elementary school in Montreal had been firebombed, and its library heavily damaged. A note had been left linking the attacks to the Israel-Palestine conflict.

The two stories and accompanying photograph about this event occupied the entire front page above the fold, and about a quarter of the page below the fold. The headline is a large banner across the whole top, something the *Globe and Mail* doesn't do very often. It has the Prime Minister proclaiming: "This is not our Canada." (If he proclaimed anything about the Pickering arson, we never heard about it.) The stories continue on page 8, occupying the entire print area, about 7/8 of the page above the fold.

Nothing more happened the next day, but there is another page 1 story on the fire, about how much damage there was and how upset it made the librarian. Page 3 provides an appropriately complementary article on how "A Holocaust victim's Bible details the horrors of Mauthausen concentration camp." The page 1 story continues on page 6; again the continuation is noticeably longer than the Pickering arson piece. There is also an editorial on page 18.

The next day, on page 19, there is a column on the incident by Margaret Wente—"Race hatred—a sign of social illness." She generously allows that, "For most people across Canada, the front-page pictures of the firebombed Jewish library in Montreal were a hard kick in the stomach." More on her anti-racism later. On Saturday, April 10, page 2 has a "Letter from the Editor", again with photo: "Book donations rise from the ashes." It talks about how librarians and schoolchildren across Canada are pitching in to restore the library's collection, and also mentions that the editor spent nine years attending the school. Apparently it did not occur to him that this might skew his perception of the event's importance.

The *Globe* doesn't appear on Sundays, but on Monday April 12 it ran a page 4 story on how "Jewish leaders applaud government's planned crackdown on racism." At the top of the comment page, A13,

# A Happy Compromise

opposite the editorials, a columnist offered a piece called "This is our Canada: We should all worry." The piece led off with references to the school firebombing and the spray-painting incident; it never got around to mentioning any attack against Muslims. The front page of the April 15 edition told us that "Fears abound at firebombed school." On the 16th, the only article on page 2 was a human-interest piece: "Young students return to fire-bombed school with grown-up thoughts."

So we have a mountain of arson and spray-painting directed against Jews, and a molehill of arson and spray-painting directed against Muslims. Is this simply a response to the current claims of an upsurge in antisemitism, or passing amnesia about racism against other groups? To find out, I checked *Globe* stories listed under the keyword "hate crimes" in my university library's database from 2001 to the present. My investigations were probably incomplete, but a couple of things caught my attention.

There are not a lot of reports specifically mentioning hate crimes. For the time period covered, Native Canadians apparently have no problems at all in this department. (Some teenagers shot up native homes with paintballs, but this was found not to have been a hate crime.) Blacks seem to be almost as fortunate: just one incident. This doesn't quite square with the stories I've heard from black people. Are they liars? Whiners? And what about other incidents involving Muslims? Was the *Globe and Mail* more even-handed?

At least no one was hurt in this year's events: not in the antisemitic attacks the *Globe* found so horrifyingly important, not in the anti-Muslim attack it found barely worthy of notice. It was not so ten days after 9-11. Here is the entire story:

> OTTAWA ONT—Police called for anonymous tips yesterday into a brutal hate crime in which a Muslim teen was beaten unconscious last week by a dozen white teens.
>
> The 15-year-old Arabic boy was riding his bicycle home in Orleans, just outside Ottawa, when he was swarmed by a group of about 12 white teens. The teens told the boy he was the reason for the World Trade Center terrorist attack and punched and kicked him repeatedly. He was beaten unconscious and left for five hours.

That's right. The incident got eighty-six words on page 10 and no,

I don't know what an "Arabic boy" is. There was, it is true, a longish general piece (757 words) on page 5 concerning the anti-Arab backlash. It does not mention the beating, just a strangling attempt against a female Saudi doctor in Montreal and some fires set at mosques and Sikh temples. (The fires had received modest coverage earlier.) The next day the beating is mentioned in a 865-word piece that made page 9. It contained Prime Minister Jean Chrétien's expressions of concern about attacks on Arabs and others.[1] This clearly did not call for a banner headline across page 1.

But fear not! A few months later, on March 23, 2002, the *Globe* did see fit to call the attention of its readers to hate crimes against Muslims, telling us that

> More than six months after the tragedy of Sept. 11, Arab and Muslim groups in Canada say their communities still live in fear. An interim report card prepared by the Council on American-Islamic relations indicated there have been 120 anti-Muslim hate incidents across Canada since the terrorist attacks. They included 10 death threats, 13 cases of physical violence and 12 attacks on mosques and Islamic centres.

That's all it said. That's the whole story. Sixty-six words on page 9.

But the *Globe and Mail* isn't against Muslims. It simply regards them, for whatever reason, as less important than Jews. What then of blacks, who are so fortunate as to have been victim to only one newsworthy hate crime?

On July 28, 2001, we learned that "On July 14, someone soaked a cross in gasoline, pounded it into a black family's lawn then set it ablaze." Someone had been charged. The quote is from a 119-word story on page 6. On August 25 there was a 246-word item about how a teenager had pleaded guilty to the crime. It mentioned that "The RCMP initially treated the crime as property mischief, due to a number of acts of vandalism in the area. But as the details of the cross burning surfaced, residents and multicultural groups responded with outrage. The Mounties quickly apologized for not treating the crime more seriously, then assigned a full-time senior investigator to the case."[2] I would have thought that worthy of an editorial, but then I don't have the refined journalistic sensibilities of the professionals at the *Globe and Mail*.

Some comment did come on September 1 in the form of a Margaret

Wente column. Remember her, the one who excoriated racial hatred this past April 8? That was racial hatred against Jews. When blacks were the target, her column began as follows:

> Memo to Hedy Fry [Secretary of State for Multiculturalism]: It's official! Someone has actually burned a cross in Canada. You've been vindicated.
> The hate-monger in question is an 18-year-old who lives in Moncton. Last month, he allegedly set a gasoline-soaked cross ablaze on the lawn of a black family in the middle of the night. The flames were quickly doused by the neighbours, and, after a storm of outrage, the teenaged boy was charged with a hate crime. Wisely, he immediately pleaded guilty.
> The kid may be just another stupid punk, but he's a godsend to Canada's flourishing racism industry, which likes to seize on every shred of evidence to prove how bad we are.

Yes, Ms Wente courageously savaged the whole racism scam, and, after dumping on a conference held in Durban, asked us to reflect: "Think what we could do if we shut down our whole government-funded racism industry." In other words: "Buncha spoilt brats, those blacks."

Having exhausted my capacity for comment, let alone detachment, I will simply end with a question. Are your newspapers like mine?

## Notes

[1] There was another passing reference to Chrétien's comments on the incident in a page 7 story on September 25.

[2] A 263 word page 17 story reported the kid's conviction on October 11.

# "Those Angry Arabs": How Canada's Media Stereotypes Arabs

## MAZEN CHOUAIB

In Canada we not only value multiculturalism, we also have policies embedded in law to support it. We not only believe that we all can live together simply through the exercise of tolerance and open-mindedness but also enjoy the differences that define who we are as a nation. To some, we are a mosaic, to others we are a tapestry, and there is a reason for the harmonious if not exquisite image we enjoy as a nation of tolerance: we represent hundreds of nations of the world within our borders through the many ethnicities, cultures, traditions, and religions that you can find in any major Canadian centre. The true Canadians are the ones who not only focus on the commonalities that we have, but also work to point these out to others, embodying the goodness of this country and its future character.

It is the encroachment of the black-and-white thinkers that threatens this uniquely Canadian cohesion. Take, for example, this dismissive statement made by an aquaintance of mine: "Excuse the expression, but he was standing in the House of Commons like an Arab beggar." This was said in reference to the position taken by a Canadian politician. On another occasion, a patron in a local coffee shop I frequent once said to the proprietor, in a voice loud enough for others to hear, "Tell your hooked-nose Arab brother to take his sign off the sidewalk." Other time-worn examples of pejorative language used on Arabs, such as "camel jockey," "sand nigger," and "desert Arabs" have surfaced in the wake of the new world order that is the post-9-11 reality. The dubious honour of being the "best" slur against Arabs today would be "Arab terrorist."

Where does this anti-Arab hate come from? Why are Arabs so despised and feared, as evidenced in their portrayal as the antithesis of what we stand for as Canadians? One might think that this prejudiced intolerance is not a trend. But ask yourself what flashes through your mind when a terrorist attack, a bombing or shooting in the Middle East, is reported in our media. Think of September 11, and of September 2000 when some Palestinians rose up against Israel in what is now called the Second Intifadah or uprising. Think of how your daily paper covers stories about "Arab violence," "Arab terrorism," and "Arab anger." Do you reserve your harshest feelings for the individuals allegedly involved, or do you form another blanket conclusion about Arab and Muslim culture in general?

The focus of this essay is media representation of Arabs and its impact on Canadians, whether they embrace Arab or Muslim traditions as a part of their identity. The media's portrayal of this community under scrutiny since 9-11 is troublesome at best, and destructive at worst.

## Arabs in Canada

The first recorded Arab immigrant in Canada was a Syrian who entered the port of Halifax, and eventually settled in Montreal in 1895. The official history of the Arab community in Canada starts at this time, according to sociologist Brian Aboud, when Canada was still in its infancy.

But anecdotal evidence speaks of others who were registered as "Ottoman Turk" because they came from territories controlled by the Ottoman Empire. The history of this community, like so many others who sought refuge and opportunity, is uniquely Canadian. Today we find many Arab Canadians bearing the names Baker, Hamilton, and other mutations of once purely Arabic names. Many Arab Canadian families of multiple generations in Canada are now substituting non-Arab names for Arab names, in a sign of the times—post 9-11 fear of unjustified scrutiny and persecution.

If anti-Arab sentiment grows in Canada, this country's system of intercultural settlement faces a death knell. Since 1961, according to Immigration Canada, immigration patterns have steadily shifted from traditional countries to African, Arab, and Asian nations. A survey conducted by EKOS in 2004 and cosponsored by the *Toronto Star* revealed that thirty-seven percent of Canadians have negative feelings towards Muslims. As many as forty-eight percent, nearly one out of two, believe it is acceptable that security officials give special attention to individuals of Arab origin.

But Arabs in Canada are the model of successful integration. This community plays a leading role in local and national politics, in the worlds of Canadian finance, medicine, engineering, academia, and the trades. Its history and culture reflect the socio-economic make up of the more than sixteen countries from where it has originated: Arab Canadians claim Lebanon, Jordan, Palestine, Syria, Iraq, Israel, Egypt, Algeria, Morocco, Sudan, Libya, Tunisia, Mauritania, and Yemen as part of their heritage. Most recently, Arabs from Saudi Arabia, Kuwait, Oman, Bahrain, the United Arab Emirates, and Qatar have come to Canada for educational purposes. They speak different dialects, but Arabic remains the dominant language. There are also many minorities within these countries that have had a significant impact on Arab culture: the Berbers of North Africa, Armenians, Assyrians, Chaldeans, Jews, Greeks, Italians, Chechens, and others have further diversified the cultural gumbo that is the Arab world: a truly multi- and inter-cultural society. Many Canadians mistakenly believe that all Arabs are Muslim, and all Muslims are Arabs. In fact, Arabs are a minority within the Muslim umma, or community.

Debunking the myths of our fellow Arab Canadians appears necessary because there is such ignorance in Canada about this community. One obvious culprit in the misunderstanding of Arabs in Canada, according to sociologist and media critic Jack Shaheen, author of *The TV Arab*, is the media. Shaheen writes that because of media portrayals, the Arab is "a made-for-TV villain, a dirty sloth, whose language is incomprehensible."

## Media: Constructing the TV Arab

The biggest offender is Hollywood. American movies and cultural products are sold around the world. So the impact of Hollywood on how our perceptions are constructed is profound and far-reaching. In the last hundred years of image-making, the Arab man has been shown as a cunning, sly, incomprehensible, and oddly dressed enemy of the straight and good. For decades, Jack Shaheen has documented these media representations of Arabs, studying and analyzing thousands of films, documentaries, and children's cartoon shows. Almost invariably, according to Shaheen, media executives perpetuated this image of the TV Arab:

> Arabs look different and threatening. Projected along racial and religious lines, the stereotypes are deeply ingrained in American cinema. From 1896 until today, filmmakers have collectively indicted all Arabs as Public Enemy No. 1—brutal, heartless, uncivilized religious fanatics and money-mad cultural "others" bent on terrorizing civilized Westerners, especially Christians and Jews. (*Seattle Post*, March 21, 2002)

*The Globe and Mail* reported in 1999 that John Larroquette, of *The John Larroquette Show* and *Night Court*, reportedly told the president of CBS: "The moment you tell me I can't slap the small brown guy, I have to go" (*Globe and Mail*, January 26, 1999). He was referring to the butt of all jokes in *The John Larroquette Show*, the inept Mohamad, who constantly endured a hotelkeeper's abuse. Here, and in so many other sitcoms, the Arab and Muslim is the object of ridicule and amusement, and Canadians are consumers of this message.

How does media representation of Arabs in America affect Canadians, who seek some pleasure in being regarded as more enlightened than their southern neighbours and able to see past these stereotyped images? Does our system of multicultural integration pass the test? We are certainly not immune to the subtle projections of bias, prejudice, and stereotyping that perpetuate racism.

## The Canadian Media

On January 14, 1999, CTV's *Double Exposure* depicted the Qur'an, Islam's holy book, as an Iraqi manual for weapons of mass destruction. This was offensive enough, but it was a Father's Day cartoon last year in the *Globe and Mail*, barely a couple of months after the invasion of Iraq, that stunned Arab Canadians. The cartoon showed, without any title or heading, the jubilation of what is supposed to be an Arab father, hook-nosed, bearded, and balding, upon receiving a bomb belt from his young son for Father's Day.

The paper's editors were surprised that a cartoon caused so much anger. The reason was simple: the message perceived by Arab Canadians was an attack on the most cherished of any culture's institutions, the family. The message, by cartoonist Tony Jenkins, was a commentary on a rash of abhorrent suicide bombings deployed by some Palestinian militants in their reaction to Israeli occupation. But in doing so, the artist, and the editors who approved the drawing, attacked the dignity and innocence of every Arab parent and child, though according to the *Globe*, the intention of Mr Jenkins and the editors was not that. The effect was. The editors refused to apologize to the community, in spite of their admission to the National Council on Canada Arab Relations and The Canadian Arab Federation that the caricature was problematic.

This incident underscored two significant points: first, it is somehow fit enough to print an attack on Arab culture and escape rebuke or reparation. Second, Arabs are gazed upon through the prism of the Palestinian-Israeli conflict.

Canadian media is controlled by an elite, members of which are products of an era that produced horrors committed on mankind and left a guilt on the West for failing to protect Jews in Europe during Hitler's reign of terror and allowing anti-Semitism to fester. Canada's media leaders, knowing that, seem to be pressed to take a pro-Israeli stance on the "Arab question." Canadian media are active participants in present-

72

ing Arabs and Palestinians as the enemy, if not overtly, than through omission or abdication of the many sides to the truth.

The CanWest-Global media empire, once owned and operated by the late Izzy Asper and now by his sons, makes no secret of its commitment to the State of Israel. An anti-Arab and anti-Muslim bias to editorial policies have damaged swaths of the community. Through its editorials, columns, and reports, many in communities of Arab and Muslim heritage have felt targeted, even blighted. Some examples from the CanWest chain are as follows:

> As George Jonas argues convincingly on the facing page, a small but substantial number of Canadian Muslims and Arabs are willing to assist terrorist operations.
>
> Editorial, *National Post*, October 15, 2001

> We have to fear our neighbours down the street . . . a degree of ethnic or religious profiling is unavoidable . . . Though few of our neighbours are terrorists, some are sympathizers. They provide the culture in which fifth columns grow . . .
>
> George Jonas, *National Post*, October 15, 2001

> We should not pretend that an effective fight against terrorism [in Canada] can be waged in a truly color-blind fashion. The fact is, those who plot the annihilation of our civilization are of one religion and, almost without exception, one race. Yet admitting this is a problem for Mr Chrétien . . . Multiculturalism is a relativistic creed that assumes all immigrant cultures are equally tolerant, civilized and enlightened once you scratch the surface . . .
>
> Editorial, *National Post*, October 8, 2001

A number of editors and columnists were sacked by the paper for refusing to comply with editorial directions to avoid criticism of Israeli policies in the occupation, and of then prime minister Jean Chrétien. Editorial independence, historically allowed to local papers to reflect their communities, was yanked from them and conferred to the head office in Winnipeg.

Describing this phenomenon in Canadian journalism, former *Montreal Gazette* editor William Marsden said, "[The *Gazette* owners] don't want to see criticism of Israel. We cannot run in our newspapers op-ed pieces that express criticism of what Israel is doing in the Middle East." A synopsis of the sinister implications of this muzzling of journalistic freedoms was best summed up by *Toronto Star* editor emeritus Haroon Siddiqui, in a speech delivered to journalists and transcribed in an article in March 2002.

> Asper decreed that editorials will be written in their head office—and must be run in all their newspapers . . . among those who did not like it was Stephen Kimber, a columnist for the *Halifax Daily News*. His column was killed. He quit in protest . . .
>
> Peter Worthington of *The Sun* wrote against all this, and his column got canned . . . another Halifax columnist got canned because he had written articles critical of the state of Israel . . .
>
> Doug Cuthand wrote a column comparing the plight of Palestinians to that of Aboriginals . . . it was killed . . . There is an irony here. CanWest are often critical of undemocratic Arab nations who practice censorship against Israel. Yet, here we are in Canada witnessing creeping censorship against Arabs . . . (James M Minifie Memorial Lecture, University of Regina School of Journalism, March 4, 2002)

## Pressure Groups

In Canada a number of organizations promote anti-Arab attitudes and disseminate disinformation. One self-proclaimed human rights organisation, in an advertisement run in a newspaper, depicted a hook-nosed, dark-skinned, balding and bearded man wearing a balaclava, holding automatic weapons, and brandishing a Canadian passport. It is a discomforting reminder of the Nazis' portrayal of the stereotypical Jewish man. Add a yarmulke and take away the scarf, the caricature looks frighteningly similar to the Nazi-era depiction of Jews. How can a self-proclaimed human rights organization, working to "combat anti-Semitism and racism" allow itself to stereotype another race and community?

Once again Shaheen describes it eloquently: "The Present-day Arab stereotype parallels the image of Jews in Nazi Germany, where Jews were painted as dark, shifty-eyed, venal and threateningly different people. After the Holocaust, the characterization of Jews as murderous anarchists or greedy financiers was no longer tolerable. Many cartoonists, however, reincarnated this caricature and transferred it to another group of Semites, the Arabs. Only now it wears a robe and a headdress instead of a yarmulke and a Star of David." (*The TV Arab*, Bowling Green, OH: Bowling Green UP, 1984)

Unlike other communities, Arabs in Canada did not pursue the protection of their culture or press politicians on uniquely Arab issues in Canada. They worked within the Liberal and Conservative parties. Over the years some Arab Canadians were elected to the House of Commons and the Supreme Court. The institutions that helped protect their cultural identity and defend their interest are a new creation. After September 11, activism among Arabs and Muslims sprouted up. This reflects a maturity and acceptance of a responsibility in Canada and for Canada.

But there is more to be done. Arab Canadians, as individuals and organizations, need to create the educational programmes that address these issues. They need to take on their civic duties within this country's social and political structures. We have to invest in organizations and institutions that can articulate our collective needs and facilitate the integration of newcomers to Canada. There is a need to reclaim the community from those who hold extreme and un-Canadian views.

Are Canadians inherently racists? Are they inherently anti-Arab? No. But many blame Arab Canadians for all the ills of their home countries. No other group is expected to "clarify their position" more than Arabs in Canada. Arab Canadians are called upon to explain the actions of their co-religionists. When someone like Osama Bin Laden, trained by the American CIA and supported to fight the Soviet Union in Afghanistan, turns against his former masters, Arabs and Muslims in Canada are expected to explain themselves and willingly submit to profiling, merely because Bin Laden is an Arab. Is it fair to label your next-door neighbour as a threat just because someone in a cave decides to blow up a tower or kill people?

Ignorance is the problem, so is lack of information. It is incumbent upon all of us to learn more about each other.

# Chasing the Dragon in Toronto, Canada

## ROZENA MAART IN DIALOGUE WITH VIDEO MAKER KAREN KEW

I met Karen Kew in the Summer of 2000, after several of my students at the University of Guelph excitedly and with grand gestures informed me that there was now an Asian woman who was the Executive Director of Ed Video, an artist-run media arts centre in Guelph. My students noted that they would now be able to enter an arts space where an Asian woman occupied a position of authority: a Media arts centre where Canadian art and culture was being produced and to which they saw themselves contributing because her presence, in their view, made it possible. "What a difference this has made to them," I thought to myself as I reflected on my own visit to Ed Video, prior to Karen Kew's hiring.

Prior to this dialogue in 2000, Karen Kew's name was brought to my attention as someone who had produced videos that depicted the experiences of Chinese and Asians in Toronto, which is where Karen lived during the early 1990s. Soon after meeting Karen at Ed Video, I took it upon myself to view her work.

I interviewed Kew on her first video, *Chasing the Dragon* (1994); my interest in it grew as I viewed it, because it spoke directly to a need that is always there within my teaching practice. When one is teaching social and political thought—psychoanalysis, political theory, feminist theory—one is often faced with the need to make theory more accessible and understandable, to be able to view cultural productions and take students through the steps of the particular teaching module; in my case, there was the reluctance of students of colour to engage with theory, often treating psychoanalysis as White and European, since many scholars and writers used European Art forms to illustrate a point. Cultural productions depicting historical periods in the lives of people of colour in Canada are few and far between, and those attempting to address questions of identity and representation in Canada are too often not reflective of the social and political climate in ways which people of colour experience it. I have found myself searching for video work in order to visually depict an era in Canadian society or Canadian multiculturalism, which I always treat a little tongue-in-cheek, waiting for students to unpack the term. So it is with particular interest that I tackle the salient features of representation within Canadian society and use the lens of the video maker to address questions of the gaze: to think about the many ways in which they see themselves, are seen by others, and are reflected within the mirror of the Canadian mosaic.

My concern as an educator is always to teach concepts, which students can utilize in their day-to-day practice as artists, writers, scholars, and intellectuals. I found with Karen Kew's work that possibility opening up even further. As someone who is schooled in psychoanalysis and also works on Black Consciousness as political practice and analytical framework, I am constantly faced with the task of bringing a conceptual framework into the broad daylight of everyday matters—the task of having to relay the significance of images, ideas, concepts, and representations into a world which defines us by these very representations, a society where terms like "minority," "visible minority," and "culture" are thrown about, especially when referring to people of colour, and where we constantly have to interpret, configure and negotiate a space to live in, make art, write and exist as Canadians.

I conducted this interview with Karen Kew as a means for us to talk about the production of her video *Chasing the Dragon* (1994) and its significance then and now, ten years since its production, in view of the fact that she has worked as an executive director for a White-dominated artist-run media arts centre. I am treating *Chasing the Dragon* as a historical production which emerged in the mid-1990s as a particular statement by a Chinese woman, a newly arrived immigrant who, mindful of the images of Chinese and Asian women flung at her from every possible source in the media, sought to produce a piece of work which reflected her analysis of her experience in Toronto, Canada.

MAART: Can we start by introducing the video and the setting? What does *Chasing the Dragon* actually mean?
KEW: It is the longing for the Motherland that you don't know, as an Asian and Chinese person. It is also the last bit of heroin, as it is sometimes spoken of in drug lingo. So it is the longing, the chasing that takes place, and since the setting is here, you can say that it is about the longing that takes place in Toronto, Canada.
MAART: Can you describe the setting—1994—and your sense of the representation of Asians in the broader Canadian culture? I think it is important for readers to get a sense of the background to the work, your own experience as a new immigrant and an artist living here, producing work here.
KEW: What struck me when I got here in 1989 was how Asians were not talking about the kinds of things that I would have imagined they would talk about. There was so much to take in. In 1989 and the early 1990s there was the whole situation facing Filipino domestic workers in Canada, the issue of 1900 numbers, the whole notion of the dial-up sex with Asian women. It was just another way of distancing yourself if you're a White man; you don't even have to face the object of your desire, you can hide behind the phone, which is really where the piece in *Chasing the Dragon* comes from, the start of the video, with the White guy Matt making the phone call and Cherry, his Asian phone sex fantasy.
MAART: The good domestic, the caregiver and nurturer, and the sexual object, the object of desire. In the case of the latter, the phone-sex connections avoided the concern with the visible, the Visible Minority

Question; now it is just about the voice, the voice that is about desire, about making your phone call, and having an Asian woman turn it into something erotic.

KEW: It wasn't just the phone sex, but also the fact that real sex trade was happening. This is the late 1980s and early 1990s we are talking about, a period in Toronto when Asians really started being desired inside strip clubs. That was when the lap-dancing thing started to happen. This is what I faced and this is what I had to deal with when I got here.

MAART: There was also the ROM's [Royal Ontario Museum's] *Into the Heart of Africa* exhibit in 1989, the same year we both arrived here.

KEW: Oh yes, I remember that very clearly. Then there was *Miss Saigon* . . . and that just did it for me; that sense of protest came out of me and I joined the protests.

MAART: And of course this was followed by *Show Boat.*

KEW: That's right. Of course, there was *Show Boat.*

MAART: Do you consider your work, or rather *Chasing the Dragon,* a form of protest? Your way of telling the society you live in, "This is what you're doing, and this is what we Asians have to say about it."

KEW: I would say yes and no. There was a sense of taking things in and thinking about what I wanted to work on, what I wanted my first piece of work to be, and also the fact that I had to work with someone, a collaborator. It was difficult to talk about the work in my class at York University, even presenting the project with people just looking at me. There were other Asians in my class, but most people did not even make eye contact. I was very surprised that people actually spoke in front of the camera and by what they had to say. Here was a group of Asians just talking about their experiences, what it felt like to be sexualized and objectified.

MAART: The focus of *Chasing the Dragon* examines, as its main theme, the gaze of White men upon Asian women. There are Asian women and Asian men, queer and gay people, and straight folks in the video who you interview, and the theme then moves to address the broader questions of sexuality, sex, and the sexual fantasy of colonial expansion brought to the bedroom of the White man. At least this is what I see and this is how I make meaning of the video. Can you say a little about your interest in doing this piece of work, and the focus you chose?

79

KEW: I had no script, I told people what I was doing, and really, other than the vignettes that were designed to bring out certain aspects like phone sex and the performance pieces which I did, which really focused on that sexual fantasy aspect, people spoke freely and spontaneously. I was surprised, because these were people I saw every day in my classes, when they did not say anything to me or to one another about their experiences as Asians. There was silence, and the minute I got the camera rolling, people just poured out the contents of their experiences, the contents of their lives.

MAART: There are some very moving moments in the video, where one of the Asian women talks about the reality of the consequences of the sexual fantasy and the implication for her in her day-to-day life. I also got a sense of the difficulty in building that sense of individuality; have you built that individual identity for yourself? I remember Fanon in *Black Skin White Masks* talking about how Black people and people of colour have been collectivized. I am interested in exploring that dynamic, how we are and have been collectivized by our colonizers, both in our countries of birth and here in Canada. Do you feel that your sense of who you are, your individuality, has been developed on your own? Do you feel that you yourself built your individual identity?

KEW: Yes, I have built my own identity for myself and I think that people do that out of a sense of having to do it because of what they face, constantly, in the mainstream media, everywhere. I think the whole piece [*Chasing the Dragon*] revolves around that, that sense of Cherry and what Cherry represents. Cherry is a total construction, a fantasy, and *is* that collective. Whereas the White man, Matt, the guy who places the phone call [at the beginning of *Chasing the Dragon*] . . . you get a sense that that is actually his real name. His individuality is present. While Cherry is a valid name, it is also that kind of Asian name, and is the sexual reference, and therefore the collective. Sangmi, one of the women in the video, talks about that, where she uses the example of the man who does not recognize her.

MAART: I thought that was a very important moment—that moment of recognizing someone, an Asian woman, as someone you want them to be.

KEW: I think that is probably the most important moment in the video; the whole interview part revolves around that moment and the fact that the other Asian women make mention of it again. I think all of us talk about that in the video. Sandy also makes mention of it, and she talks about the fact that half way through the relationship she realized that the person she was with was only with her because she was Asian . . . The hard part is realizing that in a certain way your identity is constructed and coming to terms with that, which you do, at a certain point. Then feeling that sense of grief, and realizing that it is one which you would not have chosen for yourself . . . and then that moment of realizing how to move forward with that. We all have that experience, of confronting the construction: of having men come right up to you and identifying you as someone who is their fantasy. White men would think of you in those terms, you would be named as the prostitute. I remember going into a diner and a man coming up to me and saying, "Oh, you're Lin Li." I said "No," and he said, "Yes, you are, yes you are, from the massage parlour."

MAART: Where were you?

KEW: At Bathurst and Dupont, I was in a restaurant, late at night.

MAART: So he insisted that you were someone he knew and of course as someone who had served him, and now you were sitting in the same restaurant as he.

KEW: Yes, and I thought with the insistence as well, that was something I experienced a lot . . . That is why I used the image of the geisha in another video. And it seems that this image of the geisha is carried through, over time, as though that in itself is who we are, who we can be and all we can ever be.

MAART: As a viewer, I was quite intrigued by the way you engaged with the gaze of the White man in the video. What I understood from your work, and particularly *Chasing the Dragon,* was that somehow the Master who gazes does so from the assumption that the subject has no ego, has no history except one which he depicts, which is also set against the backdrop of colonialism, and within that always as a sexualized object within the history of conquest . . . Can you say a little about resisting signification, and the manner in which the gaze of sexual and imperial conquest puts Asian men and women always on the defensive, saying who you are *not,* claiming your space, instead of engaging with questions of who you are?

KEW: Again, coming back to some of the earlier comments that I made

81

about what the women in *Chasing the Dragon* talked about . . . that
whole issue of recognition, and of being recognized as that sexualised
object . . . here, in Canada, in Toronto where I lived and where I was
studying. There is a sense in which White men may have become used
to being able to sexualize Asian women, but it's not like that anymore.
We are not a generation, despite the *Miss Saigon* image, of passive
Asian women. We are not the generation who will sit back and not challenge that gaze in our own way. We are also a generation objectifying
them as White men and White women, naming them as White . . .
MAART: And problematizing that White identity, bringing it forth even
though they may not be used to the idea of being called White.
KEW: That's right. I remember when I started my arts education here at
York. We were given a project of redoing the Mona Lisa; all we were
told was that we could redo the Western canon. I made a cardboard
cutout version, and my caption read, "Hey, White girl, what are you
smiling about?" I thought that was funny, but there was silence and just
shocked stares from the people in my class. It was okay for them to identify me, to name my identity but not for me to name them. This was
somehow problematic.
MAART: In terms of carrying out your work as a filmmaker in Canada,
what are the kinds of things that you have learnt about in presenting
your work on Identity, Culture and Representation as these pertain to
Asians in Canada? Obviously, there are shifts, with time, as one grows
and develops as an artist. I would like to hear about how these concep-
tions have undergone transformation depending on the work, where you
presented your work, who you engaged with as an artist, and your historical development as an artist.
KEW: I am no longer interested in the White gaze, and how my identity is represented by the mainstream culture in Canada. It is ten years
since *Chasing the Dragon* and I am interested in a PanAsia, in address-
ing questions and taking up concerns with a broader audience and with
a broader perspective of what Asian means—not just Chinese, Korean
and Japanese, but a broader identity of Asian and the broader significance of the gaze among one another. There is much more there for me
right now, how we see ourselves and each other, than there is with
understanding or even relating to the gaze of the White man in Canada.

# Theatre and Dissent: Waging Peace in Times of War and Media Manipulation

## RAHUL VARMA

My home town of Narion—a crowded agricultural village in the interior of eastern Uttar Pradesh, India—was informed by the richness of the shared experiences of its villagers. Life knowledge, not formal education, was its strength. I came to Canada to rejoin my family as well as for material reasons. In the twenty-five years since, I have been repeatedly asked the question:

"Why did you come to Canada?"

My answer: "To live."

And then: "Would you like to go back?"

Another short answer: "The only thing worse than immigrating is emigrating back."

And then they always bring up the matter of my Canadian Dream.

"A Canadian Dream?" I ask.

A quizzical look etches itself across the face of the questioner. It seems to say, "You came here from some place else, have become a playwright—something that you couldn't have done in your native country—and are on the radio and TV ranting about race relations whenever there's an issue; your face has appeared in the local paper, often when there is a controversy involving visible minorities; you have a publicly funded theatre company; and you seem to be a self-designated local expert on racial and artistic diversity. Isn't that evidence that you're living a Canadian dream?"

How can I respond when the things I do simply as a Canadian citizen are regarded instead as the fulfillment of my "Canadian Dream?" I didn't come to Canada for dreams. Dreams are for the sleeping. I came to Canada to be awake, to live my life and share it with my fellow Canadians, to be critical, to contribute, to belong, and to face challenges. And what a wonderful awakening it has been. One of the very meaningful parts of my journey has been the dialogue that exists between individuals and communities, even though the society itself is stratified by race, culture, and colour.

On the morning of September 11, 2001—while, by the way, I was awake, working on my script, *Bhopal*—a friend called me. "Are you a Muslim?" she inquired. "Why do you ask?" I replied. "New York is burning." What did her question have to do with New York burning? She said, "Turn on your television set." And I was asking, Why me?

That same week, my four-year-old daughter, Aliya, returned from a birthday party. "Daddy," she asked, "am I a Muslim?" I found myself on the horns of a dilemma. Whether I answered yes or no to my daughter's inquiry, the message would have been the wrong one—namely, that the tide of anti-Muslim/Arab feeling following 9-11, which had turned the Muslim/Arab identity into something to be defended or denied, was somehow justified.

In the lead-up to the US war on Afghanistan and Iraq, President George Bush Jr coined the expression "axis of evil." In an already tense environment, his statement had the effect of further pointing the finger at the Arab and Muslim communities and those who, because of their skin colour, accent, head-dress and/or country of origin, were susceptible to being associated with terrorism. My fears were well-founded. Muslim parents struggled to demonstrate their loyalty to Canada. And my daughter, like many other children across the country, from time to time—at a birthday party, on a playfield, in the schoolyard—was asked if she was a Muslim. Is she a Muslim? Am I?

The question, particularly when asked of a four-year-old child, even taking into account the horrific events that triggered it, points to Canada's racial underpinnings and to an utter lack of understanding of the geopolitical hegemony of the world's only superpower. Yet I am glad the question was asked. It opens up the opportunity to revisit this country's complex history, from the era of British and French colonization to its present state, where the postcolonial Diaspora has struggled, and continues to struggle, to arrest injurious stereotypes that single out, demonize, and discriminate people, communities, and cultures.

In his article "The Clash of Civilizations?" published in the summer 1993 issue of *Foreign Affairs*, Samuel Huntington theorizes that the fundamental source of conflicts in today's world will not be ideological or economical, but cultural. Three years later, Huntington wrote a book under the same title. In it, Huntington clumsily argues that the principal global conflicts will occur between nations and groups of different civilizations, saying that "the fault lines between civilizations will be battle lines of the future." According to him, the most dominant clashes will be between the West and Islam.

The trouble with his theory isn't only that it reduces the world into the binary of "us" versus "them" (that is, the West versus the rest)—modern versus primitive, freedom versus repression, democracy versus totalitarianism, Christianity versus Islam, etc. Huntington also grossly ignores the internal dynamics and plurality of each civilization, including the Western civilization and particularly that of Islam. He ignores the internal dynamics—the multiple competing forces among the Other civilizations—as if their people are one-issue entities preoccupied with preserving sameness. He also overlooks the historical role that countless movements have played in avoiding religious wars, defeating imperialist occupations and promoting peaceful dialogue and sharing. As if the above oppositions and historical omissions weren't insidious enough, most of the mainstream media as well as a few prominent thinkers have cited the horrendous suicide attacks and mass murder of 9-11 as proof of Huntington's theory, exhibiting outright ignorance and presuming to speak for a whole religion, civilization, or culture.

But if one were to take the internal dynamics and plurality of different cultures and civilizations into consideration, one would realize that even with the presence of conflicts and paradoxes, culture connects civilizations. This is what makes culture so compelling and complex. However, it also makes culture, particularly culture in the Third World, difficult to describe with one single definition or interpretation.

Let's look at some of the definitions and interpretations of this concept. One of the most quoted definitions—"a way of life"—is an arresting one because it may be interpreted in any number of ways. For some, the "Internet culture," whose popularity is rooted in concepts like "the medium is the message," is a way of life, claiming to connect global communities through information-sharing. The problem is that the number of Internet users and those who actually control information is miniscule next to the number of people in the world who are denied their basic human needs, much less the Internet. Information means little when the majority of the people of the world don't know how to use it. Depriving the vast majority of people of access to modern cultural goods is itself a "way of life" for global powers that greedily hold to the idea that cultural capital, like monetary wealth, must be tightly controlled rather than redistributed.

Then there is culture as in the expression "the founding cultures," which, though it sounds benign enough, often conceals a significant dose of aggression. And then there are the contemporary "multiculturalists," who view Canada as having not two but many cultures. Since the histories of the founding cultures are similar and intertwined, they are considered to constitute mainstream Canadian culture, which the remainder—First Peoples, those of mixed race, African Canadians, Asian Canadians, South Asians, Arab Canadians: those commonly referred to as the "Other"—are pressured to join. The dominant Anglo/French cultures are never asked to integrate into the Other's culture.

The slogan on the wall of the Department of Multiculturalism reads something like, "Linguistically we are bilingual, but culturally we are multicultural." Our country's make-up confirms that we are indeed multicultural, but whether our public policies are correspondingly multicultural is questionable. It is impossible to ignore the continued contradiction: despite institutionalizing multiculturalism as a state policy, Canada continues to function essentially as a bicultural country with a "multi-cultural component." This sustains unequal conditions that result in two classes of people, art, and culture—the dominant for Anglo/French (namely, the mainstream), and the subordinate for the coloured communities.

As a result, at least partially, the artistic potential of minority arts is reduced to some folkloric traditions, which too often the minorities have learned to display or distort into a form of authenticity through the costumes and customs of a remnant past, bypassing the aestheticism of the ancestral cultures from which they are supposed to have evolved. Such displays are nostalgic, not merely because of their exoticism but also because of the way that exoticism fits into the stereotype of what the visible minorities and their arts are perceived to be.

On the other hand, a definition of culture, with all its acculturation and attendant problems, as a creative framework with aesthetic gratification could magnify Canada's potential to offer endless opportunities to writers and artists experiencing the current historical period.

We are in midst of a phony war. The US and its allies insist this is a war against terrorism. But the vast majority of the people of the world believe it's a war of aggression by the world's sole superpower, which is in the habit of controlling international politics for profit. It is a racist war because it relies on Bush's doctrine that the people of Afghanistan and Iraq are incapable leftovers of the prediscovery past who must be taught a lesson in democracy under occupation. It is a phony war because it is based on lies, deception, and hypocrisy. It is a phony war launched by George Bush Jr a fundamentalist and born-again Christian who relies on a refreshed vision of theocracy, not in pursuit of democracy and justice, as he claims, but in pursuit of power, which is his masked motive. He does so in the name of the American people, implicating them in the destruction of innocent lives abroad while simultaneously suppressing their personal freedom at home.

How should the arts respond to the present crisis? The work of great artists informs us that art represents humanity's yearning to be fully human. Art attacks mental and ideological complacency, refines our emotions, and sharpens our experiences, and in doing so it profoundly honours life. So for the arts to be meaningful, theatre artists must ask an urgent question: Should they use theatre as a tool to transform theatrical actions into some form of social action in the service of waging peace in times of war, or should they restrict themselves to providing entertainment in the name of art for art's sake? With this question posed, I would like to cast a critical eye on the arts scene in Canada.

Sadly, the theatre community has never been particularly responsive to major crises, historical events, or social issues. With few exceptions, it has demonstrated a "hands-off" attitude prior to and since September 11. Major institutions such as the Professional Association of Canadian Theatres (PACT), Canadian Actors Equity Association (CAEA), the Playwrights Union of Canada, and the Canadian Conference on the Arts have not issued a single communiqué, let alone denounced the war. At the annual general meeting of PACT in 2002, I forwarded a mildly worded antiwar resolution. It was soundly defeated. The artistic director, who spearheaded the defeat of my motion, argued that it belonged to the political and not the theatrical arena.

However, theatres did respond, in other cases, to the war situation. In the immediate aftermath of 9-11, the big theatres complained about box office receipts while a letter campaign was organized pleading with the government not to cut arts funding in spite of new military "needs." Prominent personalities and institutions begged the US army to spare historical buildings, saying that once destroyed these monuments might never be recreated. Merciless bombings of people and cities of Afghanistan received less attention than the destruction of the giant Buddha statue of Bamiyan. This hypocrisy continues with the deafening silence of the Western media and the power elites over the bombing of Baghdad's national library, destroying ancient literature and the history of the people.

To top it all, the mainstream media, with its perpetual habit of strategic omission, flooded TV screens and filled the newspapers with newsy entertainment—the wonders of remotely controlled star-wars weapons, the thundering superiority of US firepower, and, to calm worried parents, the messages of "hi mom, hi dad" via CNN from sons and daughters in the "line of duty at war zone." After 9-11, a newspaper cartoon appeared showing a US soldier pointing guns at a Taliban militant, saying, "If you don't hand over Osama Bin Laden to us, we will send your women to school." This cartoon not only succeeded in bringing chuckles to readers, it fulfilled its real purpose of masking the mainstream media's hidden misogynistic attitude with regards to another culture— that if in fact the Taliban did hand Bin Laden over, the US wouldn't care if the women went to school or not.

The irony is that before US money, training, and equipment established Bin Laden as a presence in Afghanistan, girls did study and women did work. The government of the US-supported Pakistani dictator Zia Ul Haq created more than 1000 schools for zealots from which the germ of Taliban grew. The CIA looked the other way and the media turned a blind eye when Bin Laden unleashed fundamentalist violence against the Afghani people, particularly women. Bin Laden became the CIA's watery-eyed son, whose militants successfully carried out the CIA's agenda against the Soviets. I remember seeing the late American president Ronald Reagan on TV, standing in the midst of Bin Laden's fierce looking militants, saying effectively that the actions of these men were the moral equivalent of the "founding" of America. Ironically, Reagan was not altogether off the mark, since America was made possible by the genocide of its original inhabitants.

The omission of serious discussion about deadly political alliances between successive US administrations and ruthless criminals is but one small reason to question the mainstream media's attitude. Missing from discussion is acknowledgement of the political equivalence of Osama Bin Laden and George Bush Jr in their capacity to shatter hopes and destroy innocent lives serving their respective Gods, who appear to have personally blessed their missions to blast and ruin the other into nonexistence. Barring their personal family histories, their names could be interchangeable—Osama W Bush and George Bin Laden—due to the uniformity of their political crimes. Both seem to have a personal hotline to God and both believe that God gave them the sanctimonious right to commit murders—Bin Laden in the name of uniting Islamic nations and Bush in the name of "defending the civilized world." Both, it seems, have been ordained by some divine power to speak respectively for the whole of the Islamic nations and the civilized world. Both are dangerously armed, Bush with the nuclear arsenal of the obnoxiously powerful and Bin Laden with the desperate rage of the utterly hopeless.

The terrorist attack on the World Trade Centre, killing over 3000 innocent people in the name of "uniting Islamic nations," left no doubt in anybody's mind as to what the barbarism was. The retaliatory pounding—returning two entire nations to the stone age and killing over 20,000 innocent civilians in the name of "ending terrorism and defending civilization"—must not leave doubt in anybody's mind that the American barbarism is no different from the one it claims to be fighting. Huntington would have served himself better had he theorized "the Clash of Barbarians" instead of "the Clash of Civilizations." Attacks, hijacking, the bombing of embassies, and the blighting of nonconformist Muslims by Bin Laden militants is no more barbaric than successive US administration policies of blasting hopes—to say nothing of human lives—while subjugating "weaker nations."

The mainstream North American media, particularly in the US, has made it possible for its public to view other societies in terms of their usefulness or threat to America and to regard "cultural difference" as more important than the political ideas by which America judges itself. It has transformed much of the information age in which we live into a media age, in which highly advanced technology allows the nonstop repetition of politically safe information that is acceptable to the US Empire. With few and infrequent exceptions, turning a blind eye to exploitation and the subjugation of "weaker people and countries" has been a defining character of the Western media—journalistic demagogy, hypocrisy, and downright suppression of truth.

So it is not surprising that after the "liberation" of Afghanistan and Iraq, the CNN, the *New York Times*, and Canada's *National Post*, among others, haven't spared much time investigating the rise in hunger, disease, crime, and refugee crises, all of which the US promised would disappear once the bad guys were chased away. They do however bring us the good news—US multinationals have started a $1.3 million training program called "Beauty Without Borders" to "introduce Afghan women to Western-style idea of womanhood, teaching the finer points of applying lipstick, as well as other cosmetic tricks" (*Globe and Mail*, February 24, 2004, A1).

What kind of war is being waged and who precisely is represented by this enemy called terrorism? Even a neo-liberal such as celebrated writer Michael Ignatieff, who in his twisted logic supported the US "war on terrorism," has now backtracked somewhat: "How can you make war on a tactic? And if you declare war on a tactic that has proven an eternal temptation to any group that believes it lacks peaceful redress, what can victory in a war on terror possibly mean?" (*Globe and Mail*, 17 June 2004, A19).

In George Orwell's great work *Nineteen Eighty-four*, three slogans describe the society: war is peace, freedom is slavery, and ignorance is strength. The American slogan "war on terrorism" also overturns meaning. The US war on "terrorism" is the terrorism that those dependent of the US refuse to acknowledge, let alone question.

In 1988, a US missile cruiser shot down an Iranian airliner and killed 290 civilians. George Bush, Sr. commented, "I will never apologize for the United States, I don't care what the facts are." This is not merely evidence of the elitist arrogance and mendacity of a previous president, who happens to be the father of the current one. More importantly it defines a nefarious modus operandi of successive US administrations: that the facts can be whatever the United States wants them to be.

So the war has been won and no weapons of mass destruction have been found other than a couple of rusted barrels in an old shed. Here is the son of Bush again. He is unable to produce weapons of mass destruction. When asked by the media to think of any mistake he has made since 9-11, he cannot produce one of these either. And when the US Senate released the report confirming the absence of WMD, an undeterred Mr Bush simply declared, "America is safer today than it was a year ago prior to the war." How does it increase US security to bomb a country into the stone age?

Let's think about people.

For a villager in Afghanistan or Iraq whose family has died in a bombing raid, and for orphans who have never heard of the World Trade Center and have lost their parents in the ensuing wars, there is no perceivable difference between the US actions in Afghanistan or Iraq and the attacks of 9-11. However, more than a year after a war that has left yet another sovereign country under occupation, created more than 100,000 new refugees, killed more than 15,000 Iraqis (who aren't shown on American TV screens), killed over 2000 US and allied soldiers, and placed one dictator in jail, we are faced with the truth—that the US administration lied.

So why do some media sources—the *Globe and Mail* for example, Canada's respected newspaper—take a formal editorial position supporting war and the governments that support the war? Supposedly, the media serves the function of the bearer of news by extracting truth from the facts. The problem I have with the *Globe and Mail* is not that it took a prowar position even though I am opposed to the war. The problem is that the *Globe and Mail*'s position is based on naked lies.

Given media abdication of its responsibilities and governments' refusal to respects their own laws, theatre can serve alternative ways of communicating and connecting with our communities. For example, while multiculturalism provides a political climate in which overt racism and discrimination has been made illegal and punishable by law, Canada's lackluster participation in the Durban Anti-racist Conference (2001) raises questions about its commitment to cultural plurality and its own laws. Against such a backdrop, Teesri Duniya Theatre offers a theatrical response to the issues of identity, dignity, artistic innovation, and representation. The company is dedicated to developing and producing socially relevant plays that reflect the multicultural-multiracial composition of Canada and creating theatrical styles based on the cultural experiences of visible minorities living in Canada.

Teesri Duniya Theatre began in 1981 as a South Asian theatre company. Within two years, however, out of respect for the many and diverse cultural communities, the company opened its arms to artists of all cultural backgrounds. Today, Teesri Duniya has evolved into a company where artists of every culture, colour, language, and heritage work together. The name Teesri Duniya means "Third World" in Hindi, symbolizing the Third World reconstructed in the First. The company's institutional paradigm was a group of committed but professionally unrecognized artists of colour, a handful of resident playwrights and directors with stable support from their respective communities, and a strong endorsement by audiences that wanted to see the stage reflecting the social fabric of our city (Montreal). The thematic focus of the plays was the everyday cultural experiences of immigrants: institutionalized racism, exploitation, gender politics, patriarchal oppression, intra- and intercultural conflicts, and violence within and against the immigrant community.

*Job Stealer* was written in response to a 1987 incident: a boatload of Tamils from Sri Lanka swam ashore to Newfoundland off a German ship and asked for refugee status in Canada. The play propagandizes the message that the new Canadians from the Third World are merely tools in the creation of an exploitative and profitable Third World economy within the First World. The company's 1989 play, *Equal Wages*, deals with the exploitation of immigrant and refugee labour force in sweatshops, and the play is dedicated to "the struggling women of the world who have broken the silence of ages." *Isolated Incident* (1988) was written to mark the first anniversary of the shooting death of Anthony Griffin, an unarmed black teenager, at the hands of a Montreal policeman. *Isolated Incident* examined the issue of police brutality using such concepts from Indian street theatre as the storyteller, stage assistant, chorus, and street magician. *Land Where the Trees* addresses the environmental crisis caused by the James Bay Hydro Electric dam, which dispossessed the area's Cree Nation from their land. In this play, an Indo-Canadian doctor joins hands with the native Canadians, underlining the need to forge unity with the First Peoples in a common fight against institutional dispossession and cultural and environmental racism. *No Man's Land* (1992) deals with the predicament of a Muslim refugee from India who fears being uprooted for the second time by the separatist movement of Quebec. A month before the 1992 Quebec referendum on sovereignty, the Strathearn Centre (now called Montreal Arts Interculturel, or MAI) refused to rent its performance facility to Teesri Duniya on the grounds that *No Man's Land* "failed to promote intercultural dialogue." We produced the play in a garage-turned-theatre and entertained more intercultural dialogue than Quebec could handle.

*Counter Offence* (1996) presents coloured immigrants as not only racially and culturally different within Canadian society, but also ideologically different. It challenges the notion that immigrants are ideological monoliths by placing the struggle to end racism against the struggle to end violence against women. Shapoor, an Iranian immigrant, is accused of hitting his wife, Shazia. When Sgt Galliard, a white policeman, intervenes, he is accused of racism against Shapoor by a seasoned antiracist activist, Moolchand. To complicate matters, Clarinda, a black social worker who advocates zero tolerance for violence, comes to Galliard's defense, even though she knows that police violence against coloured people is indefensible.

Dominant theatre considers subjects related to Palestine and Israel as taboo, even though both of these communities constitute a vibrant part of our diversity. The Montreal premier of Jason Sherman's award-winning play *Reading Hebron* was produced by Teesri Duniya Theatre. The company's involvement in the Reading Hebron Community Project, designed by Edward Little, further demonstrates the company's willingness to intervene: to initiate dialogue between communities whose complex international conflicts have affected their domestic relations in Canada.

The company believes that political recognition of ethnicity and cultural specificity is essential to a person's identity as an individual and as a member of a group. It therefore emphasizes minority issues and focuses on minority artists while at the same time increasing interactions and exchanges with mainstream groups. Over the years, Teesri has expanded its activities to include a unique play-development program called Fireworks, under which plays and playwrights of any cultural background whose works are essentially concerned with cultural diversity are developed and showcased. As well, a theatre quarterly, *alt.theatre. cultural diversity and the stage*, was launched in 1998 to disseminate information about theatre arts and its intersection with society.

The company's latest play, *Bhopal*, concerns the explosion at the Union Carbide factory in the Indian city of the same name. It premiered in English in Montreal, was translated into Hindi as *Zahreeli Hawa*, and is currently on tour in India. The play's French translation will be produced in both Quebec City and Montreal next year. This expanded geographical mobility and linguistic range indeed signals the next phase in Teesri's life, in which the fullness of Canadian identity will be determined by a range of features—subject matter, language, audience, and the interconnectedness of different cultures—in one play.

This leads me to talk about the real weapons of mass destruction

On the night of December 3, 1984, Union Carbide's pesticide plant in Bhopal, India exploded, engulfing the city of one million in a billow of the deadly gas Methyl Iso Cynate (MIC). Men, women, and children, breathless and blinded by the gas, died like flies. That night, Bhopal became the largest peacetime gas chamber in history. Over 20,000 people have died to date and the figure is still rising.

Clear evidence linking Warren Anderson, the CEO of the now

defunct Union Carbide, to the Bhopal disaster has been disclosed and affirmed in a court of law, yet Anderson still has not been tried and is enjoying life as a free man in the United States.

If one wants to know where the weapons of mass destruction are, they must not go to Iraq. They must go to Bhopal.

That discussion was brought about in my play *Bhopal*. Just happening to premier in Montreal immediately after 9-11, *Bhopal* brought out the difference in the response to these two human catastrophes. (One can only imagine how the US would have reacted had Bhopal occurred in the US, resulting in the deaths of 20,000 Americans.) I therefore regard the play as an act of dramatic dissent designed to confront current violence through oppositional politics and creative subversion.

The explosion at the Bhopal Union Carbide plant and the attacks on September 11 are alike in that many innocent lives were destroyed. Yet the response was remarkably different, reflecting an imbalance in the way America treats the lives of its own people versus those of other people. The US carpet-bombed a country for harbouring a band of suspected terrorists; meanwhile, Warren Anderson, the CEO of Union Carbide and Bhopal's equivalent of Osama Bin Laden in terms of the death and damage he has caused, is being harboured from justice by the US. Would the US-led coalition of the willing even think of bombing America for harbouring a proven killer, let alone asking President Bush to hand him over to India for trial?

To find one man, the US attacked a whole country, and a proven killer is sitting in the US a free man. Bin Laden has a price on his head; Anderson does not. And while the response to the events of September 11 has been swift and categorical, the survivors of Bhopal continue to languish in the shadow of the modern world's most devastating industrial disaster, blocked from recourse by US indifference and faced with a future of disease and premature death. Do we need further proof that an American life is worth more than a life in the Third World?

However, in a world where industrial mass murder and wars of aggression are legitimized in the name of progress, the eradication of terrorism, the alleged existence of WMDs, and regime change, it is urgent that this imbalance be addressed in the community of nations and in the arts. As Sartre said, the theatre is the most political of the arts; we must use it with political consciousness.

In this context, artists can, of course, opt for silence and self-censorship in broaching social controversy, and produce art that is safe, pleasing, and consumable. In this case, they risk becoming ineffective simply because the bar for consumable art is constantly being lowered (as illustrated by the predominance of reality TV). Alternatively, they can engage in creative dissent, dramatizing the collision between the forces of destruction and deception and those of resistance, survival, and justice. They can articulate the horrible injustices, acts of terror, and tyrannies that plague our planet, and point a way towards redress and healing: the future of our children rests on positive action, clarity, and hope.

Clearly, the art I am advocating is not art for art's sake. Nor is it, as many would contend, an art that preaches to the converted. It is a sociopolitical response that, in fulfilling its aesthetic, influences and can potentially change the minds of the unconverted.

When *Bhopal* premiered in Montreal in November 2001, it became a forum outside the instant worldwide peace movement at a time when all discussion centred on 9-11 and dissenting or alternative voices were suppressed under the label "anti-Americanism." Supported by multimedia, displays, posters, and reading materials, the Montreal production did not shy away from what was happening in the larger socio-political context of the time.

When the play was taken to India, where it was translated into Hindi as *Zahreeli Hawa* and directed by India's premier director, Habib Tanvir, conventional theatrical practices were cast aside as it toured various Indian cities. For the Indian production, the artists, the director, and I joined people in the street who had come from all over the world to remember Bhopal. The Indian production was remarkable for Tanvir's anticolonial, pro-indigenous approach. His Hindi translation, interspersed with Chattisgarhi and English, not only propagated the language but added authenticity. It also provided native English-speakers and those who spoke Hindi and Chattisgarhi with a common ground for dialogue.

Although set in India, I regard *Bhopal* as a Canadian play. It breaks away from the excruciating stereotypes of Hollywood and colonial literature that portray Indians as exotic leftovers from the "pre-discovery" past and the whites as spiritually starved, in forlorn search of God in India. The Canadian character in *Bhopal* is a nongovernmental activist doing peace and development work, which is much closer to the reality of Canadians doing grassroots work.

During the play's initial three-night run in Bhopal itself, each performance was followed by an audience discussion. Whereas in Montreal the audience had questions, in Bhopal the audience only wanted to share their experience of the disaster—their memories of it—and they wanted those experiences and memories to somehow get into the play. In other words, the Bhopal audience saw a chance to keep the memory of the Bhopal tragedy alive, and so the play became a tool in the struggle against forgetting.

How does one find the truth when lying has become a political habit? What blame do we bear for the fates of those who suffer recurring corporate violence and the trauma of war? How can the ordinary people of the West, in whose name numerous wars of aggressions have been fought and won, coexist with the people who have been dominated, subjugated, and humiliated? Does theatre have a special responsibility for the survival of a culture, people, and civilization?

Interestingly, the parallel between the Union Carbide explosion and the war on terrorism was readily evident in the streets of Bhopal. At a rally to commemorate the disaster, posters read, "You want Osama, Give us Anderson."

For those who assign social relevance to theatre and consider it to be the humanitarian struggle of private acts for public presentation, this century has brought endless opportunities. According to Habib Tanvir's way of thinking, a war of aggression, however disguised, by its very nature is a repressive thing that sees democratic cultural expressions as antagonistic to the aggressor's culture.

The artist can draw a picture of the world in harmony with forces of resistance and survival. Artists can draw pictures of the new tomorrow as embodied in the struggle for the survival of our children.

In conclusion, the play *Bhopal/Zahreeli Hawa* affirms our common humanity and proves that, indeed, a theatre motivated by dissent is a peaceful weapon—one that is used to reshape, and not destroy, humanity. SHANTI.

# Reflections in the Mirror: In and Out of the Mainstream of Culture in Canada

## ROBIN BREON

This essay invokes the title of this book, and the metaphor contained therein as it applies to the contemporary Canadian theatre scene is apt. Art does indeed reflect life something like a mirror. But in order to capture one's reflection, one has first to be positioned in front of the mirror. Too far away or too much to the side and the mirror is unable to reflect the image. In other words, pushed too far to the margins, the mirror will not reflect any image at all. Positioned up close and centred in the mirror is the best place to be in order to see your reflected image. For African Canadian theatre artists, this manoeuvre has not been an easy one.

The complexities of racing the Canadian stage have a long history and it is one punctuated by conflict and storied by individual struggle, commitment, and achievement. Today, we are in the midst of a remark-able renaissance in African Canadian theatre. This phenomenon mirrors other recent developments in Canadian society and, although the the-atre is one of the most ephemeral of the arts, this is sure to leave a last-ing impression on our national narrative and our cultural heritage.

The Spring 2004 issue of *Canadian Theatre Review* (edited by Djanet Sears and Ric Knowles) was dedicated to the theme "African Canadian Theatre, Honouring the Word." The photographs on the cover of the journal supplied by Patricia Clark were especially striking in that they portrayed in a very graphic way, and within the same format, an ironic juxtaposition to the images that hang in the lobbies of many of the larger performing arts organizations in Canada. There you will see the head-and-shoulder shots of the artists who make up the companies for that particular season. They are almost always overwhelmingly white in complexion, with a few people of colour mixed in so that the institution can shield itself from charges that might be forthcoming from some human rights commission or urban race relations committee.

This situation is by no means peculiar to Canada's performing arts community. In a more extreme example, the *Globe and Mail* reported that the Teutonic sensibilities of the Bayreuth Richard Wagner Festival were recently offended by the inclusion of Black performers in an African-themed production of *Parsifal*.

In contrast, the cover of *CTR* included no less than forty-seven images of contemporary African Canadian playwrights, among them George Elliott Clark, Djanet Sears, Nourbese Philip, ahdri zhina mandiela, Walter Borden and many other mature as well as emerging writers. Articles within the issue covered the origin and development of Black theatre in Canada, the aesthetics of Black theatre performance, scripts, and dialogues, with regard to questions such as cultural nation-alism and the use of voice, and Black theatre in other parts of the world.

This evolution in our thinking and wanting to know more about the diasporic aesthetics of Black theatre is a far cry from the fall of 1992, when director Harold Prince and producer Garth Drabinsky announced plans in Toronto for a "reconceived" revival of the Jerome Kern/ Oscar Hammerstein II musical, *Show Boat*, based on Edna Ferber's 1926 romantic novel about life on the Mississippi. The two were unprepared for the public debate that followed on many of the same issues being discussed from a Black perspective in the recent issue of *CTR*. The debate, which burst fully onto the radar screen of Canadian public opinion, produced a catalytic dialogue on the nature of art and culture in the market place, authenticity of voice, and the persistence of racism and anti-Semitism in North American society.

The debate began when Black community organizations raised questions around the ethnocultural representation in *Show Boat*, contending that the musical historically has contained scenes that perpetuated the kind of racial stereotyping that demeans Black life and culture. Community representatives asked to be given an advance reading of the script. Prince and Drabinsky adamantly refused, calling the request censorship and an abrogation of the rights of free speech. Picket lines were then mounted in front of the *Show Boat* box office in Toronto and a "Coalition to Stop *Show Boat*" was formed. The situation became so divisive that twenty of the twenty-two members of the United Way's Black Development Committee resigned from the organization over the UW's decision to support the production by way of a gala opening-night fundraising event.

Paradoxically, a cultural dust-up had occurred in 1989 when the Jewish community raised very principled concerns over the Stratford Shakespeare Festival's planned production of *The Merchant of Venice*. The Festival responded by meeting with representatives of the Canadian Jewish Congress in an effort to facilitate discussion rather than confrontation. Central to this discussion was an examination of Shakespeare's script and the directorial concept employed in the mounting of this new production. Several excisions were agreed upon, and there was no public recrimination from the Stratford Festival attacking the Jewish community on the issue of censorship or the abrogation of free speech.

The demands made by the Jewish organizations were not treated as aberrant, anti-Christian, or antidemocratic. They were reasonable queries from an ethnocultural group that has experienced the same kind of caricature and stereotyping in literature and drama as the Black community.

By the time *Show Boat*'s opening night rolled around (in October 1993), some of the most powerful theatre critics in the US had been persuaded to travel to the newly built North York Centre for the Performing

Arts to pass judgement on the production. In an unprecedented display of unanimity, critics from the US and Canada waxed ecstatic over the $6.5 million dollar revival. At the same time, the African Canadian community was chastened by many of these critics for raising a voice against this American icon. Like cannon (canon?) fire across the bow of the Black community, the reviews of *Show Boat* were trumpeted in full page advertisements in the local Toronto press and beyond:

A Seismic Event in the American Musical Theatre . . . This version finally restores the work of its authors' original intentions in every theatrical and musical particular
–FRANK RICH, *The New York Times*

A Broadway musical that has it all! Larger-than-life performances, lush costumes, magnificent sets and technical wizardry galore! WOW!
–H.J. KIRCHOFF, *The Globe and Mail*

Impressive and stirring presentation!
–RICHARD CHRISTIANSEN, *The Chicago Tribune*

Resplendent and powerful!
–JEREMY GERARD, *Daily Variety*

A grand new show!
–DAVID PATRICK STEARNS, *USA Today*

Brilliant and marvellous!
–MICHAEL KUCHWARA, *Associated Press*

Superb and scintillating!
–JOHN LAHR, *The New Yorker*

But slowly, within this apparent wall of critical approbation, cracks began to appear. In retrospect, if one reads the reviews carefully, these same critics also express some apprehension; some nagging doubts persisted after all of the superlatives had been snatched up by the publicists for the purpose of promoting ticket sales. Frank Rich also called the production "bland," adding, "what is missing from this show is emotional punch." Referring to Edna Ferber's novel, John Lahr opined: "Certainly there's little to defend in (the) gushing best-seller on which the musical is based. Ferber writes like a teenager on diet pills . . . " And in the most unequivocal endorsement of the concerns raised by the Black community in Toronto, William A Henry III of *Time* stated flatly: "The 1927 musical is racist."

One of the strangest—perhaps surreal is a better word—aspects of the debate surrounding the Toronto production of *Show Boat* was the contention by the musical's defenders that the marginal Black characters and story line in *Show Boat* were somehow related to the history and heritage of people of African descent in North America, and that the story was an authentic and genuine reflection of this history. Drabinsky and the now defunct Livent Corporation produced mounds of press releases to this effect, along with expensive, glossy-paged "learning materials" (distributed to secondary schools) in an attempt to validate this claim.

In her brilliant monograph, *Playing in the Dark, Whiteness and the Literary Imagination*, author and Nobel Laureate Toni Morrison describes what motivated her to examine how white writers incorporate Black characters into their work: "I was interested, as I had been for a long time, in the way black people ignite critical moments of discovery or change or emphasis in literature not written by them . . . " Morrison investigates the "Africanist" presence in the fiction of Poe, Melville, Cather, and Hemingway in a dramatic reappraisal of a literary tradition built upon an equation that championed freedom and democracy while relying on enslavement and oppression as the inescapable legacy of a society built upon an ideological premise of white supremacy. She states that "the contemplation of this black presence is central to any understanding of our national literature and should not be permitted to hover at the margins of the literary imagination."

In the first years of the twenty-first century, we are still breaking out of this "contemplation" (as Morrison calls it) into the mainstream of cultural debate. The legacy of North American racialism carries with it persistent—some would say obstinate—characteristics of a racial representation that manifests itself, particularly in the performing arts, in obvious and sometimes not so obvious ways. One intriguing component of this legacy that deserves on-going examination is the continuing evolution and metamorphosis of blackface and minstrelsy.

# Reflections in the Mirror

The image of the entertainer in blackface is central to the iconography of North American popular culture. From the nineteenth-century minstrel shows, through vaudeville and burlesque, to countless films featuring Al Jolson, Eddie Cantor, Bing Crosby, and others, entertainers in blackface were a fixture on the cultural landscape.

Yet the great African American actor Ira Aldridge (1807–67) chose to live in Europe—where he became famous as a tragedian (notably in the roles of Lear, Macbeth, Shylock, and Othello) rather than submit himself to the humiliation of performing in minstrel shows in the United States. Aldridge's precedent of pushing back the colour line in the legitimate theatre of his day is now recognized as "nontraditional" or "cross-cultural" casting.

The city of Toronto had its own history of blackface entertainments, the most famous performer being "Cool" Burgess, who was the subject of a series of articles in the *Toronto Evening Telegram*. On four separate occasions in 1840, 1841, 1842, and 1843, members of the Black community petitioned the mayor's office to restrict the presentation of traveling minstrel shows that came up from the US and toured widely in Canada.

Over the past decade, a spate of books has examined minstrelsy and blackface. Mel Watkins gave us a comprehensive exegesis of African American humour on stage, radio, television, and film in his *On the Real Side: Laughing, Lying, and Signifying—the Underground Tradition of African-American Humor That Transformed American Culture, From Slavery to Richard Pryor* (Simon & Schuster, 1994). Watkins devoted several chapters to the history of blackface, from its origins with white minstrel performers to its later permutation into a vehicle for black entertainers.

Eric Lott's *Love and Theft: Blackface Minstrelsy and the American Working Class* (Oxford University Press, 1993) provided a scholarly investigation of blackface in pre-Civil War America. It examined minstrelsy as a complicated, class-based exchange founded on a mix of sincere appreciation combined with equal doses of racism, caricature, opportunism, and outright larceny. Lott's close reading of contesting dramatic adaptations of *Uncle Tom's Cabin* revivified some well-trod boards.

*Inside the Minstrel Mask: Readings in Nineteenth-Century*

*Blackface Minstrelsy*, edited by Annemarie Bean, James V Hatch, and Brooks McNamara (Wesleyan University Press, 1995), is a collection of essays that includes intriguing primary documents, first-hand accounts, minstrel guides, jokes, gender-bending sketches, and sheet music that show how blackface evolved in the mid-nineteenth century, when it reigned supreme as popular entertainment. And the fragile relationship between Jews and African Americans is explored in *Blackface, White Noise: Jewish Immigrants in the Hollywood Melting Pot*, by Michael Rogin (University of California Press, 1996), a specialized study of blackface in motion pictures since its origins, in films such as *The Birth of a Nation* and *The Jazz Singer*.

Blackface originated on the stage and, curiously, at the close of the twentieth century, it is the stage to which it returned—or in some cases did not return, depending on different aesthetic sensibilities governing a particular situation. In the decade of the 1990s, the producers in New York, London, and Toronto all had to choose whether "to do or not to do" blackface. Their solutions were as different as black and white.

*Show Boat* had originally contained a blackface routine in one of the film incarnations. The protesters in Toronto wanted assurances that derogatory representations would be cut. Director Harold Prince eventually agreed, excising the blackface scenes that had appeared in earlier versions of the musical.

Another Broadway-bound Livent production, *Ragtime*, faced the same problem when the playwright, Terrence McNally, and the director, Frank Galati, adapted E L Doctorow's novel for the stage. The novel describes the character Younger Brother's use of blackface as a disguise ("a critical moment of change" in this character's own development, to further apply Morrison's analysis) when he joins up with the band of urban revolutionaries led by Coalhouse Walker, Jr. Doctorow describes it this way: "He shaved his blond moustache and he shaved his head. He blackened his face and hands with burnt cork, outlined exaggerated lips, put on a derby and rolled his eyes. Having in this way suggested his good faith to Coalhouse's other young followers by appealing to their sense of irony."

Wisely, the creators of the musical decided that this kind of shaded irony is apprehended better on the page than it is on the stage. As was the case with *Show Boat*, they opted to cut the blackface.

In contrast, two other productions in Toronto during this period attempted to put the complex use of blackface by both white and black performers into historical perspective. Both the musical *Jolson*, a joyful celebration of the life of Al Jolson, imported from London's West End by Mirvish Productions, and Djanet Sears's play, *Harlem Duet*, made effective use of blackface. Sears's play, originally produced by Nightwood Productions, a feminist theatre company, won a Dora Award and was remounted in an expanded version last season by the Canadian Stage Company.

*Jolson* contains a scene in which the vaudeville star "corks up" to go on stage for one of his signature minstrel routines. He is at his peak, and his blackface renditions bring ovations and adulation.

*Harlem Duet* has a dressing-room scene that turns the one in *Jolson* on its ear. The year is 1928, the place a theatre in Harlem. We see an African-American actor applying black greasepaint and preparing to go on stage. As he makes up, he recites lines from *Othello*. The audience naturally assumes that he is about to take the stage in the role of Shakespeare's ill-fated Moor. Then, one final stroke of greasepaint adds a grotesque white mouth. As he leaves his dressing room, we realize in that moment that the actor was readying himself not for *Othello*, but for a minstrel show.

For the Black actor in a Harlem theatre circa 1928, the use of blackface represented a curtailment of opportunity and a diminution of his aspirations. For Al Jolson, at the height of his career in the 1920s, the use of blackface represented an expansion of the actor's talent and a chance to emulate what he called the "new rhythm" and "primitive appeal" of Negro voices.

Other examples continue to appear frequently in our popular culture. The humour in *Lend Me a Tenor*, the popular farce that has become a staple of summer stock and dinner theatres, plays upon the mistaken identity of an opera singer made up in blackface for a performance of *Otello*. Spike Lee's film, *Bamboozled*, adds several more layers of satiric greasepaint by inviting us to witness the contretemps that occurs when a depressed Black television writer conspires to get fired from an uncreative job in the broadcasting industry by putting forward the "high concept" of a modern-day minstrelsy television show that he secretly believes will be so insulting and degrading to African American audiences everywhere that the network will have no alternative but to fire him, while at the same time providing a hefty severance package that will allow him the creative freedom to take up other pursuits. Unexpectedly, the TV show becomes a big hit with both black and white audiences, plunging the writer into deeper despair.

There are other forms of minstrelsy and the emulation of black vernacular that are equally interesting from a contemporary cultural perspective. In a recent feature article in the *Toronto Star*, arts writer Greg Quill notes that Elvis Presley "was accused for decades of appropriating the music and performance style of countless neglected black American musicians who came before him, specifically Arthur 'Big Boy' Crudup."

Quill goes on to proclaim that Presley was actually "the ineffably talented but otherwise accidental by-product of a peculiar confluence of cultural anomalies . . . ," and that his voice was uniquely his own. In concentrating on Arthur Crudup, whose tune, *That's All Right Mama*, was Presley's first hit record, Quill leaves out other important aspects of the story.

It has been common knowledge in the music industry that Elvis Presley was influenced greatly by another Black singer and songwriter, Otis Blackwell, who not only wrote "Don't Be Cruel," "All Shook Up," "Return to Sender," and other songs, but also sold Elvis demonstration tapes so that he could hear the songs as Blackwell intended them.

Presley would listen to the demos and then mimic Blackwell's phrasing note for note in his performances and on his records. Elvis never corked up, but in all other respects he expropriated an African American style of performance. The fact that Presley tacked on his own name to the song next to Blackwell's for publishing credit and royalties is only indicative of the dirty dealings in the music industry during the heyday of rock 'n' roll. Perhaps it was the "confluence of cultural anomalies of the period" that Quill refers to in his article that prevented Otis Blackwell and Elvis Presley from ever meeting face to face.

In the popular current musical comedy, *Urinetown*, which (as I write) has been described (erroneously) as "the anti-capitalist" and "socialist" musical, the gospel tunes, which are placed in the second act of the show, act as a catalyst for the doomed revolutionaries who have turned to kidnapping, terrorism, and assassination in order to advance their losing cause. When I saw the production in Toronto, there was one person of colour out of a cast that numbered nineteen. The audience, too, was almost entirely white at the performance.

In this musical satire, whose humour plays upon stereotyped Brechtian tropes with references to numerous other American musicals, the greatest belly laughs occur when the ensemble parodies the movement for African American liberation with two songs, notably "Run Freedom Run" and "I See a River." The presentation style requires the actors to impersonate and physically exaggerate the vocal style and musical idiom that arose out of antislavery freedom songs and the spiritual tradition of gospel music. It was, in short, the musical's nod and homage to minstrelsy without the encumbrance of blackface makeup.

Before we go further, I think it's important to clarify the whole question of voice appropriation, whether it occurs in literature or the performing arts. And I'll leave it to my academic colleagues to translate this attempt at positionality into any of the current epistemological filtration systems that might be useful or appropriate.

In my opinion, it's probably not a good idea for artists to spend too much time on the question of identity politics and who has the right to write about whom, what, when, and where. I do believe it was good for James Baldwin to include white characters in his work, as it was equally productive for William Styron to include black characters in his. Lesbian authors may have special insights when developing lesbian characters and are also perfectly capable of capturing the heterosexual mindset, and vice-versa.

However, unlike the novel form, where many characters can exist, interact, and play roles at no extra charge to the author, a playwright needs to be judicious in the selection of subject matter and the number of characters, as well as (particularly for Black playwrights) having concern for the ethnicity of those characters, all of whom must tell their story before eleven p.m., while coming in on budget for the company producing the play.

The Pulitzer Prize-winning, African American playwright August Wilson made a strong case, in his now famous keynote address at a meeting of the Theatre Communications Group at Princeton University in 1996. He decried the present state of the American theatre, the lack of corporate and foundation support for the African American theatre movement (I would add the African Canadian theatre movement as well), and the generally limited number of opportunities that exist for members of racial minority groups in the theatre. He also denounced the trend towards nontraditional casting, saying that it obfuscated real grievances and capitulated to Eurocentrism and "imperialism" of the dominant white culture.

Wilson is right in underscoring the fact that it's simply not a level playing field out there when it comes to arts and cultural production, and it's important to vigorously critique the process at all levels.

Having said that, whither Black theatre in Canada today?

To begin, it's important to note that Canada has a long and proud history of indigenous Black theatre companies and productions. Black theatre in Canada has a recorded presence dating back to 1849, when the Coloured Young Men's Amateur Theatrical Society advertised in the *Toronto Mirror* that they would present "several scenes from Shakespeare" as well as the Restoration tragedy *Venice Preserved* by Thomas Otway (1652–1685) on February 20, 21, and 22 respectively.

Perhaps it was the legacy of this early Black dramatic society that influenced the young Ontario-born actor Richard Harrison to seek out a life on the stage. Harrison was born in 1864, the son of fugitive slaves who had fled the United States. As author and educator Errol Hill informs us in his fine history of Black Shakespearean actors, *Shakespeare in Sable*, Harrison graduated from Detroit Training School in Art in 1887 and went on to make a successful career in the theatre that eventually landed him on Broadway in the Pulitzer Prize-winning all-Black play, *The Green Pastures* (by Marc Connelly), where he played to over two million theatre goers in 1,657 performances during the 1934-35 season.

The Negro Theatre Guild of Montreal emerged in the early 1940s and was the first truly professional Black theatre company in Canada. The Guild had a lively record of production that extended over three decades.

Theatre continued to play an important role in the Black community during the cultural explosion in Canadian theatre that began in the early 1970s. The wave of West Indian immigration that came in the mid-'60s brought with it new artistic and cultural impulses that soon blended into the Black diaspora in Canada. Many talented individuals came out of this period, in particular one young black woman from Trinidad, who embarked upon the difficult journey of training to become an actress.

Vera Cudjoe studied theatre at Ryerson and took theatre and acting classes from different instructors. Although originally trained as a registered nurse in England, Ms Cudjoe wanted very much to pursue a career in the theatre. She soon found that acting is a very competitive profession with never enough work to go around, and for a black woman the road was especially tough-going. In order to open up more opportunities for black actors, Cudjoe decided to form a Black theatre ensemble. In 1973, with organizational help from Ed Smith who then taught Afro-American Studies at the University of Buffalo, Black Theatre Canada was officially launched with Cudjoe as artistic director.

The bold choice of name left no room for confusion as to the mandate and focus of the company. The first production was a play by the African American playwright Ron Milner entitled *Who's Got His Own*. Directed by Smith and presented at the Unitarian Church on St Clair Ave West in Toronto, the show's enthusiastic reception encouraged Cudjoe to pursue the theatre as a career.

The mandate of BTC did not differ greatly in substance from the mandate established over a half century earlier by the pioneering artists of the Negro Theatre Guild, which was "to establish a platform for the expression of black culture in Canada and to create an environment that could offer training to the many talented actors, performers, writers and directors of African descent who make up the black community in Canada."

During BTC's early period, a number of individuals were active in setting up the framework under which the new company would operate. June Faulkner (who was then general manager of the now-named Loraine Kimsa Theatre for Young People) assisted with the technicalities of incorporating the company and forming a board of directors. The first board was composed of, among others, novelist Austin Clark, choreographer Len Gibson, and Alderman Ying Hope. Theatre artists within the Black company who came forward to support the endeavor included Jeff Henry, Daniel Cauldieron, and Amah Harris, a recent graduate of the University of Windsor's drama department, who was interested in children's theatre and who would later found her own company, Theatre in the Rough.

It was the hope of its founders that BTC would not only act as a vehicle to share the black cultural heritage with the broader Canadian mainstream, but also encourage professional development for young artists, who would then find themselves better prepared to compete in the arts entertainment fields of theatre, television, film, and radio. To name the artists—black and white—who touched base with BTC at some point during their careers would be to construct a list too lengthy for this article. And one could also add the names of individuals who decided not to pursue a career in the arts but have gone on to success in other fields, such as community and social work, education, business, and civil service.

The body of work produced by BTC over its fifteen-year existence (1973–1988) was substantial. It is to the credit of the small, shifting staff of BTC that these mainstage productions, school tours, workshops, and classes were produced with the minimal amount of government and private support. Indeed, the organization was always precariously financed and chronically underfunded by government arts agencies. In spite of this handicap—a direct result of the institutionalized racism of the period—BTC's contribution remained steady and professional in both quantity and quality.

In the area of theatre for young people, Amah Harris initiated important work. Ms Harris began work on a cycle of plays for young people, based on the Anansi African folktales, that became the very first multiracial, cross-cultural "learning plays" to enter the Toronto school system, playing to thousands of elementary school students. Their popularity was so great that BTC was asked to tour them across the border to Detroit's Afro-American Ethnic Festival where they played to an additional 35,000 children in 1979. Also within this genre were two plays by Daniel Cauldieron, *A Few Things About Us* and *More About Me*, that emphasized the sharing of one's culture and an interrogation of the roots of racial discrimination.

For mature theatre goers there were numerous productions that introduced new plays and playwrights as well as the classics. The Jamaican playwright Trevor Rhone (*The Harder They Come, Smile Orange*) was introduced to Canadian audiences in the mid-'70s by way of his popular Kingston (Jamaica) hit, *School's Out*. The play was such a success that it was moved to the St Lawrence Centre (now CanStage's Bluma Appel Theatre) for an extended run. In 1979 Rhone mounted a play entitled *Story Oh* in a workshop production that later became the basis for his play *Old Story Time*, also a great success throughout the Caribbean and the UK.

In 1978 Cudjoe chose to mount Lorraine Hansberry's seminal work *A Raisin in the Sun* as part of the BTC season of plays. Originally produced in New York in 1958, the play had never been staged in Toronto with a Canadian cast. The production starred Jackie Richardson and Arlene Duncan and was directed by Bobby Ghisays from Jamaica. It was a critical as well as a popular success.

BTC was never hesitant about carrying forward a social and political agenda as part of their artistic work. In fact, as Black artists, they many times felt compelled to do so. The decision to adapt Shakespeare's *A Midsummer Night's Dream* and place it in a Caribbean setting was done with a respect and understanding for the important role classical theatre and classical theatre training plays in our society. Far from bowdlerizing the script, director Azra Francis (a professor in the University of Windsor's department of drama) set about to emphasize the intensely human cross-cultural potential inherent in the play, without changing one word. The production received a Dora Mavor Moore Award in the category of Innovation and Artistic Excellence and was an historic breakthrough in the area of nontraditional and colour-blind casting, which is still a relevant topic of concern within the mainstream of the Canadian theatre community.

In the mid-'80s the company helped to initiate Toronto's Arts Against Apartheid Festival, which brought to Canada Archbishop Desmond Tutu and human rights activist Harry Belafonte. During this broad-based, multi-disciplinary festival, BTC mounted the play *Under Exposure* by Lisa Evans that particularly emphasized women's struggle against racism in South African.

Over the years, Black Theatre Canada never failed in its responsibility to develop and present new Canadian plays. In addition to the plays for young people previously mentioned, a short list would include: *Layers* by Vilbert Cambridge, *Changes* by Peter Robinson, the collectively written *Bathurst Street, One More Stop on the Freedom Train* by Leon Bibb with musical direction by Joe Sealy, and *The African Roscius (Being the Life and Times of Ira Aldridge)* by Robin Breon.

It should also be noted here that Jeff Henry's Theatre Fountainhead and Clarence Bain's work with Black Theatre Workshop in Montreal initiated important parallel developments in the African Canadian theatre movement during this period, as did the Black People's Cultural Centre of Halifax with Walter Borden and others.

Today the inheritors of this legacy are continuing the work at an even higher level of artistic achievement. Obsidian Theatre, ahdri zhina mandiela's b-currents; Frank Francis and the Caliban Arts Theatre; the African Theatre Ensemble with Modupe Olaogun and Rhoma Spencer; and Trey Anthony's Plaitform Entertainment whose play, *da Kink in my hair* was originally coproduced with Theatre Passe Muraille and will be remounted as part of Mirvish Productions' 2004-2005 season—these are all continuing to produce solid work that deserves attention.

Perhaps the most significant breakthrough production in African Canadian theatre in the past decade has been Djanet Sears's play *The Adventures of a Black Girl in Search of God*. This multifarious drama, originally produced by Obsidian Theatre Company and Nightwood Theatre, employs a cast of twenty-five actors—eight principals supported by a seventeen-member chorus. With this production, Sears opened up whole new fields of possibilities for young playwrights, who previously imagined that plays could only be conceived with no more than five or six characters if they were to have any chance of making it to the stage. Not only was Sears's play produced successfully in Toronto, it was also subsequently picked up as part of the 2003–2004 Mirvish Productions season, where it ran for an unprecedented five months at the Harbourfront Centre Theatre, making it the longest running African Canadian play in Canadian theatre history.

Before continuing with the interview that follows, let me first declare my prejudice on behalf of the playwright. I have known Sears for over twenty years. We originally met during my tenure as administrator and associate producer with Black Theatre Canada in Toronto (from 1981 to 1988). Djanet (who then went by the name Janet) was a young woman with a driving curiosity who wanted to know how the theatre works. Even then she was gifted with an abundance of creative energy and a ferocious intellect. If BTC (which closed its doors in 1988) mounted a poetry workshop, Djanet had a poem; if we organized a music workshop, Djanet had a song; and when we put out a call for auditions, Djanet was first in line.

I asked Djanet about her experience in mounting the inaugural production of *The Adventures of a Black Girl in Search of God* with a brand new theatre company.

Says Sears: "I just have to say that the pressures of launching a new play with a new national company, and with a very large cast, [required] an extraordinary effort that carried with it great risk for all of us. Unlike other companies where success may rest on a season of plays —our entire *raison d'etre* rested on this one event. The fact that we were successful was wonderful and very lucky, at the same time let me say simply: had we failed, we never would have received a second chance."

*The Adventures of a Black Girl in Search of God* is a morality play that deals with faith and spirituality while including a neat subtext of Black history, ethnocultural representation, and the nature of relationships. It has substance as well as style, form as well as content. The premise of the play is simple and taken from a story that surfaced in newspapers several years ago. It seems that the local town council up in the rural northern community of Holland Centre, Ontario, wanted to change the name of Negro Creek Road. They didn't like the word Negro, thinking that it was old-fashioned and a bit insulting to Black folks. They wanted to change it to Moggie Road in honour of an early white settler.

The small local Black community, whose ancestors go back to the days of the Underground Railroad, when fleeing Black slaves found sanctuary across the border in Canada, rose up in protest. Sears saw a drama unfolding in a little community and wound up writing a play that asked big questions.

Why did she think this incident had the stuff of drama in it? Sears begins by choosing her words slowly and carefully, and then rushes into the answer as her thoughts and ideas begin to speed up. "I followed the story in the papers and then didn't think too much more about it. But for some reason it wouldn't leave me. Then about the same time came a huge controversy at the Royal Ontario Museum in Toronto concerning their exhibition of African artifacts entitled, *Into the Heart of Africa*. The curator mounted the exhibition and interpreted the artifacts through the voices of white missionaries of the period. It was meant to be postmodern, with a heavy sense of the ironic. The irony was lost on many members of the black community in Toronto. There are a few lines in the play taken almost verbatim from the exhibit."

What happens in her script is a fictional conflation of these two events, which become thematic throughout. "I believe in my heart that stories are a fundamental nutrition for the soul," she continues. "These stories are everywhere, in the news—wherever—and so I tried to approach this play as having several layers of stories to tell."

Sears also directs her play, and in authoring the production as well as the script, she takes on significant challenges. I asked her how, in constructing her story, she arrived at the idea of a chorus within the structure of the play. Was she harking back to the Greeks?

> In a kind of Aristotelian way I wanted to create a vehicle, not to advance the narrative so much in any neoclassical sense, but to advance the unity of action within the play, and so I decided on the use of a chorus, which one doesn't see very often in contemporary North American plays. It really comes more out of African story-telling techniques, constant movement, gesture, dance and sound—reaching as many of the senses as possible, sometimes without the audience even being consciously aware of it.

And what does she think about authoring a play that has met with such popular and critical success? Djanet Sears does not take the honour lightly.

> As an artist, I constantly think what a privilege it is to be able to work in the theatre. There are many things that differentiate the Black experience in Canada and make it unique. To be part of this creative pulse that articulates and gives expression to this experience is a great gift— and a constant challenge.

The resilience of African Canadian theatre artists has demonstrated that they will not fail to meet the challenges that lie ahead. In his engaging account of Montreal theatre from 1920 to 1949, entitled *Setting the Stage*, theatre critic Herbert Whittaker observed: "In any country, no matter how thinly populated, no matter how widely scattered across a continent, people must eventually produce their own theatre, as objects on a landscape must produce their own shadows." Or perhaps they must seek out their own unique reflections in the mirror of our national art and culture.

# The Theatre of Racism

## ROZENA MAART

Life is the non representable origin of representation
JACQUES DERRIDA

To frame an art piece is usually the task of the creator.

To hang it for exhibit, in a public space, becomes the task of the curator. To stage the production of racism, on the page, the white page, for the Black writer who takes pleasure at being both theatrical and theoretical, takes a little bit of courage and a lot of determination. Yes, determination, I tell you. For the written page is almost always crafted out of a determination . . . to record, whether for the purpose of memory or the sheer desire to tell the story, because, if not spoken, it has to be read. The act of racism I lay bare to you here is, after all, a comedy of errors. Whatever the errors, the mistake can also lie in viewing racism as simply a straightforward matter.

Telling the tale of racism is firstly the prerogative of uttered speech, for in this act lie my consciousness and politics. Writing follows speech and my concern when writing, when recording the tale of White domination, is always with the scene of writing, with the inscription of textual lines. My process of inscription is one where I let blood lines and textual lines meet—this is the aim of the exhibit I display here—transmitting the echo of my blood and fusing it with my written word—it is here where the Whiteness of the blood (of the agents of White domination) meet the Blackness of my text; it is here where the Whiteness of the artist claims and reclaims the space of Art and Culture at Ed Video in Guelph, as a White space. Ed Video . . the Regional Centre, away from the flux of migration and immigration and hence not a threat to the White geography, so beautifully imagined, in the absence of ghettos, in the absence of Black presence forging representation in the White city, not only through restaurants, but through Art and Culture, quite against the better wishes of Empire builders chiselling away at sculptures destined for White-owned galleries, viewed by people of colour who now grace the cultural corridors of Guelph. It is here, on the white page, beyond the anaemic flesh that enters the mainstream white text, that I visibilize White presence; it is here beyond the unnamed flesh, the unnamed agency which bears White Consciousness, which writes its White presence as an absence, that I make it present; it is here where the textual line as boundary exhibits yet masks the ideology of White domination, which I, in turn, erode; it is here that I stage the theatre of racism as carried out by the agents of White domination, those performing it, inflicting it, perpetuating it, reproducing it, in the name of the White father (the guardian of the White nation) and the White mother—the bearer of White children for the nation; it is here where my Black Consciousness exhibits their racism and confronts the blood which flows through invisible veins, as silence: a silence which guillotines Black presence. The deed has been done, they have removed Black people and people of colour from their Art space, a former slaughterhouse. If that is not an anaemic irony, both comical and disturbing, then it is the fact that the funders spearheaded the vulgarization of their racism. You may sit back now. My Black blood will leak onto the white page; the bleached, formatted page. The door to the theatre has been shut. The frames are now being stacked for exhibit. You may read, in whichever order suits you best.

It is a theatre that is not disseminated by speech . . . but by the written word and the dissemination of written documents. It is a modern-day theatre, a theatre of cruelty, where speech is absent and tragedy lies in the cowardice of the flesh, of the absence of uttered speech in the flesh; the usurpation of space, the cruelty of coloniality, is staged in writing: signatures are accumulated, young boys are solicited, brought off the streets by White mothers . . . write thy name on this, I say to thee . . . look at me . . . this is my body, my blood, given to you and to many. . . do this, sign this, in memory of me . . . go in peace and serve your Whiteness . . . . When signatures are accumulated, are gathered together, in one name, to remove Black presence, that act is in the name of racism.

The scene of the crimes . . . the telling of the tale . . .

A White man, employed at an Artist-run Media Arts Centre shows *Birth of a Nation* as a teaching video and disregards the authority of the Executive Director, who asks him not to show the film; he does so anyway. He dismisses the guidance provided to him by the Executive Director, a Chinese woman, whose superior British education extends further than the White settler-colonial arm of anyone employed at the Centre, despite the actions of those whose ignorance bespeak their desire to continue the colonial legacy left to them by the Mother country, England. A White woman anoints herself with the title of "Artistic Director." She does so because she can; she is robbed of the possibility of being the authority in an Arts Centre where a Chinese woman is the Executive Director, and she therefore has to Christen herself, the only strand left to her to assert her Whiteness and ensure that the followers of White Christian domination will now speak on her behalf, since her White knights have overlooked her desire for recognition. Her anointment ensures the possibility of her ushering herself further into the Centre with a title, and have this title stand as testimony to her use-value, not exchange value, for in her determination to resurrect herself she overlooks the possibility that her presence is not justified, not with the value with which she has embraced it. Her Christening is a lavish ceremony, demonstrative and wordy, a distasteful and boastful display, for now she can partake in the joy of being someone: someone with a title. She soon realizes that despite her title, she still has to take direction and guidance from the Executive Director; knowing full well that the organization has a hierarchy and that she, unlike what the racist society around her suggests, is not in charge: she is not the Jane of the White jungle . . . and no, she does not have paid subordinates either. At numerous occasions, she proceeds to slander members, making statements about their personal lives, many of which, if uttered could have resulted in lawsuits and she is asked not to repeat this kind of behaviour. Yet, she refuses; she writes retractions upon retractions, the violence, hissing through each letter she crafts to complete the sentence. In ceremonial folly she proceeds to repeat the very pattern of behaviour she has just asked to be excused of, in writing. A second White woman, in her desire to make decisions for Black people and people of colour, rejects the notion that members of an Artist-run Centre should not screen *Birth of a Nation*. She speaks of voting, voting on whether White Supremacy should be screened, on that White canvas, that White screen.

Former Prime Minister Jean Chrétien, on the televised White screen, insists, "the majority cannot make decisions for the minority," . . . and on the other side of the colonial coin, this White woman tosses the idea, stomps on the coin and insists that democracy of the Volk should reign . . . preaching the ethics of fairness to the dark and the colourful . . . insisting that the members should have voted on whether *Birth of the Nation* should be screened. The birth of this Nation, the history of the Ku Klux Klan . . . saluting the new direction, the new democracy, in White reprise, without a pause, is redeemed as the instructional, the educational/certified by the University of Ignorance and Arrogance, a lethal, colonial combination, submerged in floundering egos and floating phobias.

TO BE CONTINUED!

But the Black South African president, the Colombian Board member, and the rest of the Board, decide to suspend the membership of those who have sought to undermine Black presence. Black presence signifying authority . . . your membership has been terminated . . . cut . . . there is no entry for the Volk, so determined in forging ahead with White Supremacy. Their actions against the Board and the Executive Director are called to a halt . . . you are not permitted to exercise your racism here . . . if you understand this basic requirement, you may participate within the parameters laid out in the mandate.

It is a theatre where the unspoken theme is blood . . . fluidity . . . sexual relations . . . relations of the blood: of founding fathers, the one who writes to the women of colour and demands his right to be considered, for he speaks on behalf of his Volk, who in turn rely on him to erase the women of colour from their Arts Centre. It is then on behalf of the mothers that he writes his scathing letter, demanding that his Whiteness be upheld . . . those women of colour have forgotten their place, they need to be reminded of it . . . he writes his violence, in a letter, on behalf of the mothers who are held in regard for their ability to reproduce for the nation; it is in their name, the name of the family who is related by White blood, White sweat, White tears, the fluidity of White motherhood—tears, milk, and blood—that White domination is sought and maintained; it is for the continuity of the Volk who cannot be shamed out of representation because Black people and people of colour occupy positions of authority; it is the continuity of the mythical notion of community, fuelled by the desire to keep it as White as it used to be . . . that the wronged White woman instructs White men to fight for her, to fight in her name . . . in the name of the White children she has borne for the nation, their Volk.

The crimes of racism are never told in full. The crimes of racism, when told, become the suspicious lava of an outpour of White guilt to the White reader whose consciousness is pricked in poetic prose, for the appeal has to be made on the level only the poser understands. A consciousness of consideration emerges for those whom the story-teller reveals. It is often the seduction of the written word that arouses moral sentiment, the act of racism itself, lost, forgotten, between the twenty-six letters of an alphabet which cannot speak its name, cannot write the deeds . . unnamed . . . denied . . . extracted from the written word . . . rendered absent . . . insignificant. It is after all a White page, why contaminate it with unspoken truths! With Black ink, my writing reveals the actions of White folks, so determined in their ability to silence Black people, silence us in every way, even in the telling of their racism. And since, in the language of racism I inscribe, there is neither victor nor victim, the significance of the tale itself is subject to scrutiny, a reader has the privilege to pick and poke at, question, interrogate even, for the crimes of racism are hidden, the telling of the tale forbidden. It is from the forbid-

# The Theatre of Racism

den that I write. The forbidden of where, how and on which grounds a Black woman writes the realities of racism so many experience within Artist-run Centres in Canada. Shall it be just a simple telling? Shall I reveal the full details? Or shall I mask, protect, and shield the perpetrators from the warfare of the written page, that as a textual guerrilla I perform as passionate textual politics?

Should I name these agents, these actors of racism and White domination, inscribe their Christian names, or shall I refer to them as nameless and identify them by their actions, which bear their names—by their ability to ensure that White domination is upheld and perpetuated. I have no fear in calling their names, writing their names, representing them by the names they were given, Christened with . . . for it is in the signing of their name that they resurrect White power. A naming reveals who the person is . . . allows the reader a familiarity and a particular distance: the known provides the moral ground to stake the distance, the distance is one of privilege, where the reader can savour the knowledge of who the perpetrator is and single her out—and say, Oh, I know her, it is not me—while overlooking the act/s. There appears, often, too much interest in the person, the one named by her racist actions, for the interest in understanding racism is often in pathologizing the act or the actor—he is just a little crazy—a silent moral gesture which distances the reader from the perpetrator; or the stamp of class prejudice—he is White trash and therefore not mindful or intelligent enough to mask his racism—a comfort with the naming of White when depicting the lower classes of White intelligensia. For the learned perpetrator, the Artiste, it is the quiet pleasure of not being named, and this she cherishes, the quietness of not being named. Talking about racism, naming racism, is only the prerogative of the suffering underclass, and naming the perpetrators as White only belongs to the poor and the lowly; it is thus in the silence of the violence of her acts that she lives, in comfortable Canada. The White reader, concerned, troubled by the racism of others—it is always others, never him—in not knowing her name does not have the privilege of peace of mind, but has the responsibility of interrogation, self-interrogation. I shall refrain from citing her Christian naming—I shall name her by her actions, as an agent of the system of White domination, the characters she occupies within the fairy-tale of racism. Knock . . . knock . . .

Snowhite and the thee little pigs are at the door. . . shall I let them in?

The violence of the letter . . .
 The written letter is not harmless; its intent, when accumulated as the signatures of the Volk, is not to harm, not to bruise or graze but to destroy—to eliminate—those people of colour and restore White authority: the presence of those whose signatures speak as Volk. The violence of the letter has its pens hanging, swinging swiftly in the breeze of death and elimination . . . leaking its poison. The petition is not harmless, it is a violence, a letter as White letter, as ultimate White penship, injected with White poisonous ink . . . clustered around the White nipple—calling for the resignation of the Executive Director, a Chinese South African woman, calling the Board of Directors unlawful—not lawful, not in a position to uphold the unspoken law of White Supremacy. The letter ruptures, the letter carves, the letter posits the seeds of cruelty and destruction. The letter, written by one, written by many, disseminated, its seeds blowing in the gentle wind of Guelph's cafés and bars; the letter as petition, as the signatures of the Volk is sent to a higher authority, the funders of the Volk. The Volk gathering of signatures; the "concerned artist" did not sign his name, for in the absence of his name he swore his allegiance to the system of White domination. The authority is not in the name, not in the listing of the name, but in the signature, the final mark of White authenticity, which instigates, instructs, demands . . . the removal of the disapproving.

The crisis of representation is when White artists are faced with the prospect that White domination will be contested and challenged. Three people of colour do not echo the concern. The crisis is the myth of White mythology being toppled by the authority of coloniality; if anyone has that authority, it was the British-educated women of colour. White mythology is the belief that White culture and the interests of White culture will be represented—for one White man on the Board signifies that departure, and not even by any knowledge of his convictions, but what they believe is the conviction of another White man who has challenged the strength of Whiteness, their White Mythology. Of course, a White man cannot stand up and fight racism or challenge White Supremacy, he has to be led astray by a woman of colour. The crisis occurs when the represented do not represent those for whom representation means Empire and White domination, with the certainty of continuity.

The petition is a graceless manoeuvre . . .
   The privilege of the signature is not that it will be seen, but that it will be heard—by White ears—such is the expectation of racism: to have the ears and eyes of White authority, the only authority tuned to their signatures . . . to have the funders read their signatures and respond, as though in the signing of their names, lies the crisis. Look, here lies my name . . . I sign my name to this petition; I demand that you listen to me and act on my behalf. This is my signature, I summon you to act on my racism. This written document is the sum of my grievances, my signature makes my grievance legal. I am important because I have signed my name, and in the signing of my name, lies my importance. The written paper, when signed, represents the authority of White presence, which has been rendered insignificant. It is not presence that the agents of White domination want at Ed Video, but White presence. The petition is a graceless manoeuvre, an act of cowardice, for it calls for the removal of people of colour, for whom the word *representation* apparently holds no representation. As people of colour, we are the represented—we do not represent—we are what caricatures are made of. We are not meant to hold or represent authority of any kind except in areas of the exotic or erotic— the theatre of chopping and cutting, of flavouring food, of the libidinal theatrics of sexual pleasure, jumping and dancing, the spectacle of being looked at—and in silent, blissful, gratitude, we are meant to accept this offer of peaceful coloniality. You, Black woman, you exist, but according to me. I, Snowhite, summon you. Snowhite, I do apologize for my dignity and my authority—I learnt it from my ancestors. In my veins their blood still rebels; in my jaw the roar of the lion sleeps in cheeky repose.

In a Canadian culture where Art has meant the reproduction of European art in every possible form, the Black woman, the woman of colour, exists as the subordinated subject of the White gaze. The colonial postcard depicting the African market with Black women, in abundance, carrying buckets of water on their heads, bare-breasted and all—for the White Artiste this is called Art; the White Artiste for whom the pornography of the poor tickles, titillates. There is also art which depicts sexual tourism—a cheaper version of the Gauguin fairy tale. Fantasy is fantastic; it is not a crime. A crime cannot be committed in the imagination of the imaginer, even if the subjects displayed in the imagination are docile, exotic creatures existing only for his pleasure. The problem with fantasy is that it leaves the mental screen of the imaginer unexamined and becomes the basis for her or his interaction with the Native, the woman of colour. A silent performance on the mental screen of the imaginer is the setting for the theatre which unravels as the White man and the White woman come face-to-face with revolutionaries who out them, remove them from the protected pedestal of penile puerility, take them to task on their performance of racism—that which they name Art.

The Vulgarization of Racism . . .

In the footsteps of the White man who has been removed from his position where he enacts racism, new ones have to be made. He fears them fading, with little trace remaining that he has been present. The smell of his racism will leave. If he is left astray, with no deposits of racism to make in strategic spots where his racism can grow, infect, and inflict, he will be lost. His public drinking house . . . the ebar . . . the university . . . the bookstore . . . the tea rooms . . . the café . . . he marks his territory, drags his petition to every possible spot. When Black women and women of colour are instrumental in his removal, he will fight back, only to assure them that he has more avenues available to him than their knowledge of his racism allows . . .

*Der Spiegel* . . . *The Mirror* . . . The Newspaper as ideological apparatus. *Der Spiegel* praised its artists . . . Wagner was glorified. The local newspaper is sought to stage yet another act of Volk solidarity. The suspension of artists is not a news bulletin, not worthy of local or national importance, as the petition is initiated and circulated by six White folks seeking the reinstatement of White privilege and White power. The newspaper as apparatus fulfils its duty, is instrumental in promoting the theatrics of the artists wrapped in the denial of their racism. Racism— the eye-catching title, whose significance as an act, an atrocity, as violence is not detailed; it is a title, given to Knighthood, expelled by the tongues of those for whom spoken truths are forbidden fruits.

The suspension of privileges is treated as a castration. They are cut off from the artery of White power, because the Arts Centre, their production house of White dominance, has cut them off, has castrated them; they can no longer thrust their White power. When reality fails to correspond to the desired ideal, castrated and defeated, they will turn to the violence of the letter—the petition, the electronic mail delivered to the doorstep of the White Knight. It is a citizenship of common blood—mourning, tragic, public. The limp White penis is in remission—its owner will erect his White kingdom through his battered ego, through his wronged self, and stroke himself publicly . . . a masturbation of loud angry cries, caressed by the one he identifies as Oedipus, whose simple life is one of tragedy. When castrated blood gathers together, in one name, in the name of the castrator, they erect the cross of White power and call it by another name/ Art.

Being under erasure . . .

The defeated Being, the Being that exists under the threat of caution and erasure. If I had to wear a sign on my body, indicating that I have been eliminated from the Board of Directors of Ed Video, this is most likely what I would look like—crossed out, eliminated, axed, lynched and still hanging. A defeated Being is the best evidence that racism exists and that its force has destroyed even the littlest rebellion—especially one staged by Black women and women of colour. It is the rope, the cross, the stamp, the axe, and it is under a state of caution that I would exist within a place where my presence would be thwarted. A Being under erasure is what the colonial seeks to maintain. The Native has ninety-five percent of his people killed, the remaining five percent a reminder to him of their death. The Being which exists as a Being under erasure, a Being destroyed, erased, eliminated, is a Being which gives testimony to the acts of racism—the acts of humiliation and destruction.

# Do Foes of Gay Marriages
# Simply Fear Joy?

## TAREK FATAH

A husband and wife celebrate their twenty-ninth wedding anniversary. Last month, we attended a number of weddings in Toronto. Each had its own flavour, from Pakistani to Palestinian, from elaborate orthodox church ceremonies to modest mosque rituals. Though the rites differed, the grooms and brides were all beaming with joy.

As these couples embraced their future together, we couldn`t help but feel sad for Canada`s gay and lesbian couples who are being pilloried for seeking the same happiness. We were also transported back in memory to a humid August evening in Karachi in 1974 when we were permitted to marry by our parents after a great deal of initial resistance.

Gays and lesbians wishing to marry face a gantlet of opposition and we, as a heterosexual Muslim couple, can empathize with their pain. To become husband and wife, we too had to confront deep-seated prejudices.

126

Culture, religion, and family would not permit the daughter of a Shia Muslim of Gujarati ethnicity to marry the son of a Sunni Muslim of Punjabi ancestry.

Four years earlier, our paths had crossed at a noisy demonstration at the University of Karachi. Two twenty-year-olds, us, pursued graduate studies in English literature; one an orator with two stints as a political prisoner, and the other a Beatles fan with a Ringo Starr mop of hair who had never been to a protest rally in her life. They fell in love. In true Islamic tradition, she proposed, he accepted.

However, it was not to be that easy. This was in traditional Pakistan where nothing happened without parental assent. When news got out that Nargis Tapal and Tarek Fatah wanted to wed, all hell broke loose. Both families vetoed the match. Devastated, we contemplated eloping. We were accepted at Oklahoma State University for graduate work but just to get there would cost a fortune, and we were penniless.

With nowhere to run, we persevered and several years later, both sets of parents buckled and gave their consent. To this day, we still cannot understand why it was so difficult to achieve such simple joy. After twenty-nine years as husband and wife, we want no one denied the happiness that we enjoy.

Sadly, the gatekeepers of bliss and the purveyors of grief are still alive and well. From prelates and imams to rabbis and pundits, the forces of religion are arrayed against the gay and lesbian community. Once again, we are witnessing an attack on joy and happiness in the name of religion and tradition.

As practising Muslims, we acknowledge that no faith, particularly Islam in its traditional interpretation, permits same-sex marriage or condones homosexuality. However, neither does faith allow hate and bigotry to be camouflaged as a quest for religious purity.

Most Canadian Muslims reject the notion of same-sex marriages and they are perfectly entitled to their beliefs, if, indeed, the issue is one of belief. But we think the position taken by religious leaders attacks the basic humanity of gays and lesbians. Dehumanizing them is the first step to setting them as targets of bigotry and hate. Invoking religion to accomplish this task is shameful.

A Muslim monthly magazine asked its readers in an editorial, "Would you rather have church or state in your bedroom?"

Without answering the question, and oblivious to the implications of inviting church, mosque or state into his bedroom, the writer goes on to predict moral disaster.

Accepting homosexual relationships as "marriage" will be the last nail in the coffin of human morality, according to the editorial. "We Muslims allowed and promoted the delinquency in our daily life and kept quiet; we tolerated the illegitimate relationships of consenting adults outside marriage; we turned a blind eye to the 'coming out of the closet' and hid behind the curtain of 'hate the sin, but love the sinner'.
. . Even if we are looked upon in the West as 'fundamentalists' or 'homophobes,' it is an obligation for all Muslims to do our part just as the Catholics are doing," the editorial added.

Last nail in the coffin of human morality?

Not the Holocaust, not the genocide in Rwanda, not the massacres in Bosnia? Just same-sex marriage? Not murder, not hunger, not rape, not war, not honour killing, not illiteracy, not sexual assault by clergy, not its cover-up? To the editorial writer, nothing seems to be as vile as homosexuality.

Muslims should know better than to fall into this trap. They have been at the receiving end of slander and hate and it has taken collective action of some courageous people to defend the human rights and humanity of Muslims as equal citizens in our society. Even though an overwhelming majority of Canadians does not believe that the Qur'an is word of God and Prophet Muhammad, may peace be upon him, is a Messenger of God, we Muslims have been given a status, at least in the law, as equal citizens, no matter how offensive others may find our religion.

The same holds true for the other side. After all, Muslims do not believe that Jesus was Son of God or that God should be worshipped in physical depictions such as statues, or that God does not exist at all, as atheists say. However, not only have we learned to accept Canadians with whom we have profound differences of religious belief as they are, we have also developed a society in which these differences are no hindrance to our relationships with each other.

It has been the intrinsically tolerant nature of Canadian society that has defined the rights of Muslims as equal citizens. How should we then campaign against the very values that accord us the dignity we deserve?

If you believe your religion doesn't permit gay marriage, then simply don't marry a person of your own sex. End of story. Why would you wish to impose this standard on people who believe that religion, in their interpretation, does not exclude same-sex marriages?

The same religious groups that today hypocritically say that their only objection to the proposed law is the word "marriage," were at the forefront of challenging Bob Rae's Bill 167 in 1994, a proposed law that did not mention same-sex marriage but spoke only of same-sex marriage.

The law drafted by the federal government as presented to the Supreme Court makes an explicit declaration protecting the right of any church, mosque, synagogue, and temple to refuse to perform same-sex marriages.

So why the fuss over gay marriage? Could it be that the same forces of religion, tradition, culture, and hate that opposed our heterosexual marriage thirty years ago are still making their presence felt? Is it joy that they fear? Happiness, it seems, is an affront; they simply cannot fathom the idea of two people wishing to live together as a family, and to be accepted the way the Almighty created them.

As a happily married Muslim couple who had also experienced resistance and opposition, we need to speak on their behalf. If gays and lesbians wish to pursue their own path in life, who are we to place obstacles in their way? If their choices are contrary to that of the Divine, only the Divine can be certain. Let us discover God in our kindness and compassion instead of hate and self-righteousness. For isn't God the most merciful and the most compassionate?

Only God knows whether we are right in standing up for our gay friends but we do so in all sincerity and with the hope that no one should shower grief over the happiness sought by another human being. Let us learn to live and let live.

# Youth, Diasporic Identity, and the Politics of Representation

## Chelva Kanaganayakam

On July 11, 2004, the *Toronto Star* carried a feature article entitled "One Weekend, Many Sides," subtitled "Different reactions as youth search for identity in the midst of western culture." In the process of creating a narrative through a series of interviews with Middle Eastern and South Asian youth, the reporter comes up with several observations about cultural identity, all of which are somewhat flawed. First, the idea of conflating Middle Eastern and South Asian youth is in itself a homogenizing gesture that erases significant differences between communities. The assumption appears to have been that they are all immigrants and brown and must therefore have a great deal in common. The author, San Grewal, is hardly aware of the sheer Orientalism of his description: "The young and old, all from Toronto's Arab and Persian communities, smoke shisha pipes and pour liquor from bottles sitting atop the tables as they watch people get drunk with joy on the dance floor . . . Then a belly dancer floats around the cavernous, smoke-filled room for half an hour" (B6). Having thus contextualized the night scene that draws the youth together, the author drives home his point that while all of them wish to get what they can out of Canada, they are committed to returning "home," since home is where values can be preserved. There is, for instance, the following statement by a student from Pakistan: "I'm going to go back to Pakistan—I don't accept the culture here. If I don't protect my culture and keep away the negative values of this culture, then how will the children? My friend has been totally absorbed into Canadian culture. He has no respect for his parents. He even swears in front of them. My aim is to get my Master's degree here and then go back." The constant motif is that "routes" have failed and that "roots" have endured.

Two days later, in response to this article, Maneesha Mehra writes: "We do not intend to go 'back home,' because this is our home. Instead, we have taken our deep-rooted respect for the values, beauty and richness of our South Asian heritage and blended it with the values, beauty and richness of Canadian society and made this our 'home'" (July 13, A 19). As a celebration of a hybrid identity, the rejoinder is predictable. In the process of empowering herself and her community in this manner, Mehra points to the ambivalence of "home" that continues to be an issue. It also draws attention to the notion of return as an alternative that she chooses not to entertain. In some senses, the statement legitimizes and valorizes the Canadian mosaic and the multicultural ideal of distinctive identities within a unified national imaginary. Home and diaspora merge in this reiteration of empowerment.

The feature article that offered a reading of youth through what was ostensibly an objective and empirical study received much greater space than the subjective response of one individual. The dichotomy between the two drives home the politics of representation as a crucial element in the national imaginary. In a country where diversity has become the reality, is there a disjunction between what happens in everyday life and how it is imagined in the media? There are, of course, no easy answers, since much of the evidence that is gathered tends to be anecdotal. Even so, the fault lines are often visible. Media representation of minority communities tends to be minimal; and when there is an attempt to highlight minority presence in the city, the impulse is to exoticize or essentialize the present in ways that imply and promote marginality rather than belonging. For the most part, there is a refusal to recognize that immigrant groups tend to construct their identities in complex ways. On September 25, 2004, for instance, the Tamils in Canada gathered together at Queen's Park to express a desire that the Canadian government take a more central role in resolving the ethnic conflict in Sri Lanka. Conservative estimates say that approximately 50,000 people gathered for four hours to express their solidarity and their desire to promote greater Canadian involvement in Sri Lanka. The next day *The Toronto Star* carried no write up about the gathering or its significance. It is the failure to treat that moment as important in any way that is striking. Where representation projects a particular version, what is lost is the complexity and richness of a whole society in transition. A simple binarism effectively blocks out the possibility of understanding contexts that need to be looked at carefully.

At some level, identity politics revolves around Canadian multiculturalism, since that is a defining feature of Canadian policy. The much-flaunted "mosaic" is not entirely a figment of the imagination, and it certainly plays an important role in defining national identity. Here again, there is no consensus, no easy way of determining how it works in practice. Even a cursory look at the books by Neil Bissondath, Arnold Itwaru, and Suwanda Sugunasiri reveals that there is no agreement among critics about the virtues of multiculturalism. The fact is that the immigrant presence is such that one wonders about the term "visible minority," certainly in urban centers such as Toronto. Surely, if the Tamil community alone could publish three telephone directories for itself, multiculturalism, at least in terms of demographics, can hardly be disputed. The University of Toronto claims that forty-two percent of its students are non-white. Multiculturalism is thus very much a reality, although still a problematic one. In practice, the centre and margin tend to remain distinct categories, while multiculturalism serves as an ideal to allocate spaces within the margin.

In 1997, Mitra Sen produced a short film entitled *Just a Little Red Dot*, which became an instant success. The story of an adolescent immigrant girl from Sri Lanka, the film traces the initial resistance of the school children to the "otherness" of the girl, the timely intervention of a teacher, the gradual support of a few children and the transformation of the school as everyone learns to accommodate and welcome change and diversity. Set in Toronto, the film offers an idealized and often benign vision of a multicultural society with the metaphor of a bindi or red dot becoming a symbol of unity across races and ethnic groups. The film works with a version of political correctness, a kind of liberal acceptance of otherness, that is as comforting to the immigrant as it is to the mainstream community. The film specifically targets a young audience and is intended to be tendentious.

I have argued elsewhere that the film projects a multicultural and national myth. At a time when several national myths appear to have become obsolete or irrelevant, the myth of multiculturalism ensures the significance of citizenship and nationality. But that is a far cry from belonging, from an ethos that paves the way for a sense of rootedness. There are many issues in the film that are deeply problematic. The central motif itself needs to be looked at carefully, since a religious symbol is secularized and made the basis of commonality. The film glosses over the competing claims of nationality and belonging, and it de-emphasizes the dichotomy between acceptance and assimilation.

The fact is, however, that the film has had an amazing after life. The cool dot club, which consists largely of the children who acted in the film, still continues to promote the film, involves both youth and adults in discussions, and in general promotes the vision of liberal acceptance. The popularity of the film is a reminder that some aspects of multiculturalism do appeal to the youth and that the notion of reaching across ethnic and racial boundaries is not without some measure of validity. The film is to a large extent a kind of wish-fulfillment, a feel-good cultural presence.

The reality, however, is far more complex. One of the questions that we probably need to ask is whether such questions about identity, culture, or memory matter in any significant way. And this is not intended to trivialize the question or adopt a fatalistic stance that since there is probably not a whole lot we can do to alter the march of the present, we might as well go about our business. It is equally possible to claim that these concerns are not new, and that in different historical contexts, similar problems have been raised and resolved in many different ways. Take, for instance, *Othello*, or *The Merchant of Venice*, and you find a complex study of outsiders desperately trying to hold on to a way of life that are seen as unacceptable. If the Jewish diaspora or the Africa diaspora are not, in any fundamental way, different from what we are experiencing today, then should we not direct our energies to understanding what happened in the past rather than reinvent the wheel? More to the point, are issues such as identity, ethnicity or any such grouping ultimately obsolete in the context of a relentless and ever-expanding globalization?

In that sense to talk about identity is in some ways a reactionary stance. And certainly, to insist on a nativist or purist stance in a diasporic setting is much more of a reactionary gesture. We recognize and witness the inevitability of change and the consequent loss of cultural memory. With every passing generation the changes become more evident, a process that we tend to call assimilation or integration. The gradual attrition of language, the tendency to change or shorten our names, are all clear symptoms of both assimilation and globalization.

On the other hand, it is possible to argue that in some ways we will always remain the "Other" in the same way that Shylock or Othello was an Other. Multiculturalism implies a mosaic, but in practice it does not negate the binarism of mainstream and margin. I do not wish to imply a hegemonic model, but rather that as far as multiculturalism becomes another way of implying tolerance, differences will remain. In practice, the idea of a mosaic is deeply problematic, since equality of cultures will constitute a babel of sorts. If Canada has two official languages, then multiculturalism must imply something other than the existence of a constellation of cultures within a magic circle.

Once we agree that in terms of classification, the notion of minority communities will remain, then the issue becomes one of representation, and conceptualization. The two intersect in significant ways but are not similar. Representation here refers to a system of signs that we employ in order to project ourselves as distinct ethnic communities. Our representation is often shaped by how the nation configures itself. The values that are stated or implied in Canada as a secular, democratic state are echoed in the way we respond in relation to the mainstream community. Representation here implies both how we tend to project ourselves and how we are represented by others. These are both very significant in relation to how we might imagine ourselves into existence. The point I am trying to make here is similar to what Edward Said made in relation to the Orient.

In Saidian terms, minority communities have been imagined in a particular kind of way. The historical circumstances that necessitated certain events and the movement to the West, the ways in which they have been defined, have to do with the manner in which they represent themselves. Periodically, they are described according to certain modes which then become normative. Fiction then becomes fact as communities shape themselves according to the ideology that shapes them. In any analysis of minority communities this aspect of constructedness needs to be considered seriously. New groupings such as East Indian or South Asian now become operative, and groups tend to imagine themselves in such ways. We see the expression of this sense of solidarity in our prejudices and biases.

As we also know, the Saidian model is less than perfect. It tends to homogenize a complex historical process and it tends to construct a simple binarism based on hegemony. A number of recent studies have shown the need to reshape and finesse the argument to understand structures of control. Power and influence are not necessarily one-way streets, and there is always a complex configuration of assimilation and mimicry. It is, nonetheless, true in a general sense that once communities are imagined in a particular way, and a particular construct is held in place by a pervasive institutional system, it is often difficult to think outside that frame.

That form of representation can be very different from the way in which we conceptualize identity. There are of course two obvious obstacles to the process: one is that of homogenization. Any generalization is likely to be a simplification of sorts, given the many differences that exist in terms of regions, class, religion, etc. These have their roots in patterns of migration, in colonialism, in historical circumstance. Even within regions, the differences are sometimes so remarkable that any monolithic reading is likely to be flawed. The idea of a Sri Lankan, for example, is varied, fluid, and multiple. The moment we define ourselves according to a pattern of inclusion, we begin to respond in ideological terms.

The second obstacle is the tendency to essentialize a culture. Particularly in a context where minority culture is considered to be at risk and sees itself as beleaguered, the temptation is to let nostalgia construct a wholly distorted version of "home" and its way of life. The fear of erasure or contamination is a significant factor in creating an imagined past and then replicating that in the present. The immigrant communities themselves thus become participants in a process that constructs a culture which has no roots in the remembered or adopted country.

At the same time, the notion of "home" is for minority groups, in one form or shape, a major concern. And that is more than nostalgia or memory. Their investment in the political future of the country they left behind is much more than perfunctory. Regardless of political stance, the fact remains that for many immigrants the concern with the political situation at "home" is immediate and relevant. One aspect of this visceral link is that the events in the home country have had a direct bearing on the people who moved to Canada. The second is an economic one, made possible by the relative prosperity of this country. The need to reaffirm one's status and sense of belonging by showing an excessive interest in "home" is also part of immigrant sensibility.

Another aspect that is equally important is that we need to see immigrants in Canada as creating distinctive cultures in their own right. There is of course much greater hybridity here than at "home," particularly if home tends be, in racial terms, quite monolithic, and that is obvious in the acquisition of language, mannerisms, etc. But it is also much more than that. There is the question of adapting one's customs, conventions, and beliefs to a new environment that insists on its own codes. Ritual, for instance, changes when conditions do not allow for replication. And when rituals change, a way of life also changes.

The point that needs emphasis is that we cannot make the assumption that the manner in which immigrant communities define themselves is sufficiently inclusive or even accurate. As far as they were part of a community that shared their beliefs there was really no need to attempt a definition of what it meant to be part of an ethnic, religious, or racial group. When they felt beleaguered they needed to establish a form of solidarity, but that did not necessarily involve a process of interrogation. The challenge then was of a different kind. Now having become a part of the diasporic community, there is a need, not only to understand the past, but also to review it critically. In short, the idea of an immigrant community in Canada is not a given. The exercise is not one of remembering and recording how they lived and what they valued. They need to undertake that with a measure of self-consciousness about the various intersections that made up immigrant or minority culture. There may be aspects that they are not particularly proud of or wish to continue. But they may well have been part of the fabric of their life and cannot be wished away.

When dealing with the present, there is also the need to recognize that the past cannot be replicated. Notions of space, of public and private space, secular and sacred space, have altered in a Western context. Together with that, relations between men and women, between parents and children, between the rich and poor have undergone changes. What happens, for example, when a rural framework gets transformed into an urban setting? What one decides to foreground here may not be what was privileged at home. These changes are inevitably cultural. No immigrant community can be seen outside the framework of that transformation.

And that is another way of saying that in some ways the immigrants in Canada have a measure of autonomy. How they understand themselves has much to do with how others understand them. And that is never an easy task. Among classes, between generations, within regions, there have been identifiable changes. As far as communities think of themselves as immigrants or exiles, they will remain on the margins, not only in relation to home but also in relation to Canada. Peter Shalk has written a book about the Sri Lankan immigrant community in Stockholm in which he provides a photograph of the current Hindu temple there. Juxtaposed with that photograph of an apartment building in which the temple is housed, is another picture, of a grand Hindu temple in Sri Lanka, which, in ideal circumstances, the priest would like to emulate. The two occupy two ends of a spectrum. One is the ideal and the other is the real. It is important to relate to the temple in Sri Lanka in order to historicize the present; but it is equally important to study the present in order to understand the present and shape the future.

What is quite striking, however, is the kind of fundamentalism that one encounters in the various communities, particularly among the youth, in the recent past. If "fundamentalism" is too strong a word, at least a kind of defiant assertion that is in stark contrast to the synthesis of multiculturalism. In the Greater Toronto Area, this kind of resistance has gathered momentum over the last several years. Interestingly, it

takes the form of an essentializing discourse that celebrates a remembered culture or an adopted one. In recent years it is possible to see
among the youth a strident desire to proclaim a "native" identity that
may well be an abstraction rather than a lived experience. Asserting an
identity, real or imagined, in ways that display distinctiveness entails a
curious ambivalence. On the one hand, it allows for solidarity; on the
other, if the symbols are not organically connected to the lived experience of the youth, that leads to a state of confusion. The fact is there is
a much greater assertion of solidarity, often on the basis of religion.

One of the reasons for this form of nativism could well be that recent
patterns of immigration have increased numbers to a point that offers
the possibility of communities living together and not having to interact in any significant way with other groups. Another would be that
global and transnational conditions promote certain ideological stances.
As global situations harden along racial or religious lines, the effect is
felt among the youth, whose loyalties tend to be inherited rather than
acquired. More importantly, there is the issue of representation in the
media which also creates a backlash among youth. There is, in the
media, a consciousness that given the demographics, some representation of visible minorities is necessary and inevitable. When it occurs, it
unfortunately reiterates an Orientalist discourse. Classical Indian dance,
exotic customs, etc, get reported together with violence and lack of
moral standards. Commercials hardly ever depict South Asians. In keep-
ing with political correctness and a commitment to multiculturalism,
when South Asians do get introduced, it is usually in small roles, where
they come across as functionaries. The dichotomy between the distribu-
tion of the population and the representation in the media is thus a matter of policy and ideology. As the media, consciously or otherwise, mar-
ginalizes minority groups, the tendency is to increase resistance with
assertions of "native" identity.

In general terms the issue of representation is a troubling one, and
on occasion it has led to deep divisions. The exhibit *Out of Africa* that
took place in the Royal Ontario Museum in Toronto a few years ago is
a case in point where representation led to considerable unpleasantness.
South Asia has occupied a somewhat ambivalent space, particularly
after an imagined India became fashionable, with people buying T-
shirts featuring Ganesha and lunch boxes advertising Krishna. A rough

estimate would be that there are 1.5 million South Asians in Canada, a country of 30 million people. And media representation does not do justice to the presence of such a large population. One of the consequences of the absence of such representation is both the marginalization and homogenization of communities. East Indian thus becomes an all-purpose term that includes everybody. Such a flattening of differences also has the effect of creating social structures that are not mindful of differences. In turn, that feeds into the identity politics of South Asian youth, who are confronted with images that are at a remove from the reality they encounter. For the most part, South Asians remain unaffected by the images that appear in the media, but such images do affect mainstream perceptions of the community.

Representation might well account for some manifestations of ethnic identity. But they do not fully explain the kind of preoccupation with "home" among the second generation in ways that are counter-intuitive. There is, for instance, the Tamil Students Volunteer Program (TSVP) , which organizes annual trips to Sri Lanka where young undergraduates devote the entire summer to volunteer activities. They obviously feel comfortable in such surroundings, since the program itself is a huge success. What is striking is that the youth feel the need to go to a country that they had never really known. The people, rituals, customs, and values are to some extent alien to them. In fact, language is often a major hurdle since the youth is hardly competent in local languages. And yet they feel the need to return, and do so with a sense of accomplishment. It is said that the Sri Lankan Tamils alone have some 150 associations based on Sri Lankan villages, institutions, and other special interest groups.

It might well be that Sri Lankans have a very specific history of immigration that accounts for some traits. It is quite likely that Indians or Pakistanis may not respond in quite the same way. But it is naïve to accept the practice of multiculturalism without careful analysis. On the one hand, youth tend form larger affiliations on the basis of colour, religion, or language, thereby circumventing the claims of nationality. On the other, differences between countries do matter, and they need to be acknowledged in any study of identity politics.

It would be equally idealistic to imagine that "home" would provide a total identity to diasporic youth. It cannot, simply because root metaphors do not travel well. Dipankar Gupta makes an interesting argument about root metaphors and spatial configurations. He excludes diasporic communities from his matrix. It is possible to argue that first-generation diasporic communities do retain some sense of root metaphors. For the second and third generations, such metaphors become distant. Landscape, ritual, and space, for instance, get configured very differently in diasporic settings. Sacred and secular spaces take on a different dimension in Canada. For the youth, that might well constitute a problem. At one level, the assertion of an "authentic" identity is seen as a counter to the hegemonic gestures of the mainstream community. At the same time, authenticity is hardly possible in a land where the land imposes its own set of definitions.

Hybridity, from the perspective of identity politics, thus becomes a reality at this juncture. The hybridity that *A Little Red Dot* advances is based on compromise and accommodation. That is closer to adjustment for pragmatic purposes. When a new set of conditions intersects with remembered values, the transformation that occurs is probably a truer kind of hybridity. In that sense, hybridity needs to be seen not as a fusion of two cultures so much as a new set of markers negotiating the values of another culture.

Here one is reminded of a recent essay written by the Sri Lankan Canadian writer Shyam Selvadurai, entitled "Summerscapes." As the writer travels up north to cottage country with his partner, he is reminded of the fact that he too had a history of holidays. Now while his partner enjoys a history in the artifacts and in the landscape that is available, he bemoans the fact that he has been cut off from those sources of enrichment. At the end of the essay, he says that, since he has been going to cottage country for several years, he too has symbols that establish a past, he too has a landscape that retains a sense of meaning. "With each year, I saw the progress of my entries from unfamiliar to familiar to taken-for-granted; a growing knowledge of my landscape.

As I looked around the room, I found other evidence of my presence—a pair of fire-engine-red slippers, bought in Chinatown for $1 . . . acid-washed jeans from my club days, turned into cutoffs, and then just abandoned . . . One book held a photograph of me in my old favorite swimming trunks; on the back, a friend had written 'f.y.i., Speedos went out in the 80's.' . . . I had been so caught up in the past, I had not realized that this Canadian holiday home held my history too." In short, Selvadurai attempts a personal history rather than a collective one, in order to establish a sense of identity. He does not jettision his Sri Lankan identity, but realizes that new narratives need to be told.

There is, of course, a dichotomy between the private and the public. Selvadurai attempts to solve a personal crisis of sorts. For the youth as a whole the symbols may have to be more collective. If, for instance, urban space imposes its own norms, then there is a need to reconcile the new values with a culture that is neither entirely familiar nor entirely alien. The challenge is an important one, and it is evident in the way culture evolves and even in the way writers write. It is possible to speculate that the paucity of second-generation South Asian writers is precisely because the challenge to create new metaphors to depict old values is a daunting one.

Amita Handa, in a book that deals specifically with South Asian women, speaks about the need to "negotiate all these contradictions by articulating a third position of subjectivity, one that is neither traditionally Canadian nor South Asian but speaks to the fluidity of categories." She adds: "There are extreme emotional costs, however, in negotiating fluidity. The effects of this fragmentation—the constant hiding of selves, the feelings of shame that this can elicit, and how this affects all aspects of self-esteem—still remain untheorized" (166). In general terms, it is possible to extend this argument to both men and women, particularly the youth. By the same token, it is possible to argue that new opportunities offer new possibilities for defining culture, and particularly in countries such as Canada, there is a much greater degree of empowerment that allows for much greater latitude and freedom. As we think about identity politics, particularly in relation to youth, we need to understand, in complex terms, the ways in which they conceptualize their world view. It is now becoming increasingly clear that it is simplistic to assume that time will erase the past and lead to assimilation with the mainstream. Instead, there might be a hiatus, followed by a resurgence. In fact the youth may well prove that it is the older generation, which surrounds itself with images of a remembered past, that is confused and dated.

Whether it is the youth or the older generation, the fact remains that patterns of immigration, multiculturalism, identity, and representation are all unstable terms that have the potential to fragment the national imaginary. In countries such as Canada that allow and need large numbers of immigrants, any form of cultural stasis is hardly possible. At the same time, diversity cannot eclipse the need for some form of cohesion that functions on the basis of a centripetal focus. The relation between the acceptance of diversity and the promotion of national unity has at least in part to do with the politics of representation that perpetuates hegemonic myths. Instead of recognizing the multiple layering that is germane to immigrant identity, representation often flattens differences to project a vision that is binary, unequal and simplistic.

## References

Bissondath, Neil. *Selling Illusions: The Cult of Multiculturalism in Canada*. Toronto: Penguin Book, 1994.

Grewal, San. *The Toronto Star*, "One Weekend, Many Sides," July 11, 2004.

Gupta, Dipankar. *Culture, Space and the Nation-State*. New Delhi: Sage Publications, 2000.

Handa, Amita. *Of Silk Saris and Mini-Skirts: South Asian Girls Walk the Tightrope of Culture*. Toronto: Women's Press, 2003.

Itwaru, Arnold Harrichand and Natasha Ksonzek. *Closed Entrances: Canadian Culture and Imperialism*. Toronto: TSAR Publications, 1994.

Kanaganayakam, Chelva. "Cool Dots and a Hybrid Scarborough: Multiculturalism as Canadian Myth." In *Is Canada Postcolonial? Unsettling Canadian Literature*, edited by Laura Moss, 141-148. Waterloo: Wilfrid Laurier Press, 2003.

Mehra, Maneesha. *The Toronto Star*. July 13, 2004.

Said, Edward. *Orientalism*. New York: Random House Press, 1978.

Shalk, Peter. *God as a Remover of Obstacles: A Study of Caiva Soteriology Among Ilam Tamil Refugees in Stockholm, Sweden*. generUppsala, Sweden: Uppsala Universitet, 2004.

Selvadurai,Shyam,"Summerscapes," http://www.nytimes.com/2004/07/05/opinion/05SELV.html

Stevens, Paul. "Globalization, *The Merchant of Venice* and the Work of Literary Criticism." Unpublished article.

Sugunasiri, Suwanda. *How to Kick Multiculturalism in Its Teeth.* Toronto: Village Publishing, 1999.

# Contributors' Notes

NURJEHAN AZIZ was born in Tanzania and came to Canada from the United States in 1980. She cofounded the *Toronto South Asian Review*, later the *Toronto Review of Contemporary Writing Abroad*, and is the publisher of TSAR Publications. She is editor of the anthologies, *Her Mother's Ashes and Other Stories by South Asian Women in Canada and the US* (1994), *Her Mother's Ashes 2* (1998), and *Floating the Borders: New Contexts in Canadian Literature* (1999).

SHARON MORGAN BECKFORD is a PhD candidate in the Department of English, York University. Her research interests include African diasporic, Canadian, postcolonial, and Native literatures, as well as Black cultural and feminist studies. She is currently involved in research at the Centre for the Study of Black Cultures in Canada at the Robarts Centre for Canadian Studies, York University.

ROBIN BREON is an arts and cultural journalist who has published in a wide variety of both popular and academic journals in Canada and the US. A founding member of the Canadian Theatre Critics Association, his work has often commented on equity issues as they affect the arts community.

MAZEN CHOUAIB is the executive director of the National Council on Canada Arab Relations (NCCAR) and a commentator on Canadian foreign policy in the Middle East.

JUNE CHUA grew up in Alberta and is currently a writer living in Toronto. She has worked as a reporter, producer and writer for the Canadian Broadcasting Corporation (CBC) in radio, television and online. Her work has been published in the *Globe and Mail*, *Canadian Living*, and *Scarlett*. Her "Cafe Chat" columns can be viewed on CBC.ca.

TAREK FATAH is the host of the weekly TV show, *The Muslim Chronicle*, and a founding member of the Muslim Canadian Congress.

CECIL FOSTER is the author of a number of novels, including *No Man in the House* and *Sleep on Beloved*, as well as *A Place Called Heaven: The Meaning of Being Black in Canada*, and *Where Does Race Not Matter: The New Spirit of Modernity* (in press). He is an assistant professor at the University of Guelph.

CHELVA KSANAGANAYAKAM is a professor, at the Department of English, and Director of the Centre for South Asian Studies, at the University of Toronto. His publications include, *Counterrealism and Indo-Anglian Fiction* (2002), *Dark Antonyms and Paradise: The Poetry of Rienzi Crusz* (1997), *Configurations of Exile: South Asian Writers and Their World* (1995), and *Structures of Negation: The Writings of Zulfikar Ghose* (1993).

ALNAAZ KASSAM is a high school teacher in Toronto. Her academic education includes a BA from McGill University, and a bachelors, masters, and doctorate in Education from the Ontario Institute for Studies in Education at the University of Toronto. She is currently working on issues of literacy, technology, and identity retention for minority peoples.

KAREN KEW, a graduate of York University in Toronto, is an artist and video-maker. She has been the Executive Director of Ed Video, a media arts, artist-run centre in Guelph, Ontario, since 2000. She coproduced *Chasing the Dragon* (with Ed Sinclair) and has made other videos, many of which are distributed through V-Tape, in Toronto. Karen Kew lives in Guelph.

ROZENA MAART, a Black South African, came to Canada in 1989. She took her doctoral degree at the Centre for Contemporary Cultural Studies at the University of Birmingham, England (1993-1996). She is a professor, a writer, and does psychoanalysis. Her areas of work are Black Consciousness, psychoanalysis, Derridean deconstruction, feminist politics, and political philosophy. She lives in Guelph.

ARUN MUKHERJEE teaches postcolonial literatures, predominantly South Asian and minority Canadian, at York University in Toronto. She is the author of *Postcolonialism: My Living* (1998, TSAR). She recently translated, from Hindi, Dalit writer Omprakash Valmiki's autobiography *Joothan* (2003, Samya, Kolkata and Columbia University Press, New York).

MICHAEL NEUMANN is Professor of Philosophy at Trent University. He is the author of *The Rule of Law: Politicizing Ethics* (2002) as well as articles on such topics as rights, utilitarianism, Rousseau, and rationality.

FRASER SUTHERLAND was born and raised in Nova Scotia, and has lived in Montreal and in Nelson, British Columbia. A writer and lexicographer residing in Toronto, he has published twelve books. His most recent poetry collection is (with Goran Simic) *Peace and War.*

SANJAY TALREJA is a filmmaker who has worked in the visual medium—primarily documentaries—for a number of years in India, Canada, and the US. He is also Assistant Professor teaching documentary and media-related classes at the University of Windsor. He is presently working on a documentary on cricket in Toronto, and his documentary *The Rise & Fall of Bombay* will be completed by Fall 2004. He has a MFA in Film from Ohio University and bachelor's degrees in law and commerce from the University of Bombay.

RAHUL VARMA is a playwright, essayist, and community activist. He immigrated to Canada from India in 1976. In 1981, he cofounded Teesri Duniya Theatre and has been the company's artistic director since 1986. To advance the company's mandate, he launched the theatre quarterly *alt.theatre: cultural diversity and the stage* in 1998. His full-length works include *No Man's Land*, the radio drama *Trading Injuries*, *Counter Offence*, *Bhopal.*

Society and the Language Classroom